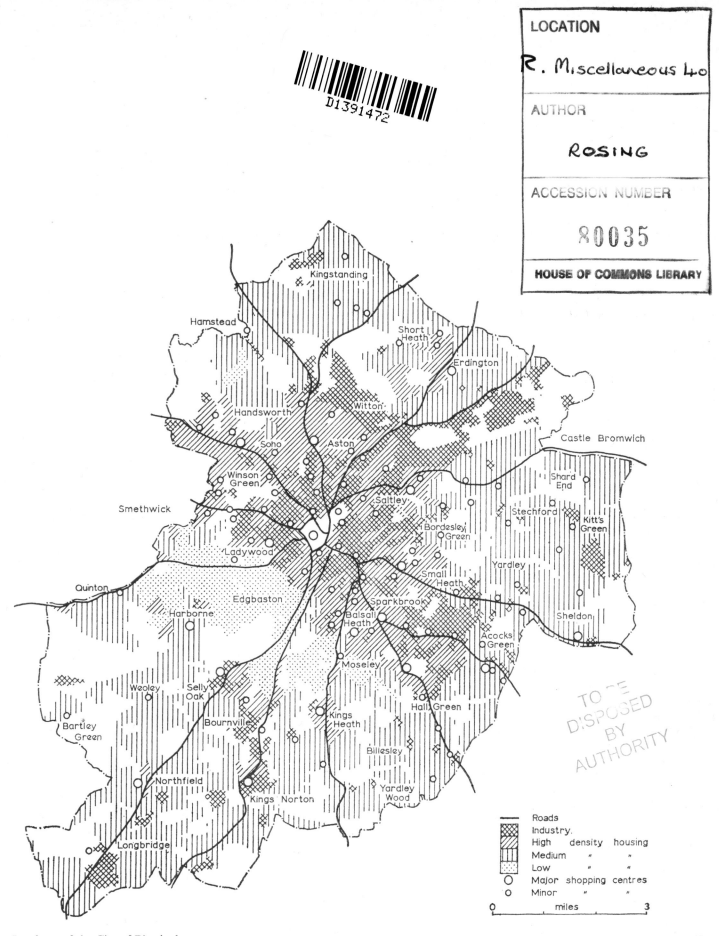

Roads
Industry.
High density housing
Medium " "
Low " "
○ Major shopping centres
○ Minor " "

0   miles   3

Land use of the City of Birmingham

Character of a Conurbation

The West Midlands Conurbation is one of the classic areas of mixed urban and industrial development established during the Industrial Revolution. Twenty years ago it had been the subject of several pioneering planning studies and its problems were widely discussed and appreciated. Since then, population growth and migration, insufficient and obsolete housing, industrial changes, the expansion of service and office employment, higher living standards and the motor vehicle have intensified the difficulties of planning this great urban complex. Today, once more, regional planning is a live issue and yet in the West Midlands the intervening period has contributed little that is new in detailed information about the region's problems.

This atlas provides a uniquely detailed presentation of the facts about the Conurbation in the form of computer maps, with statistical analyses and commentary. The source of information is the 1966 Sample Census, using enumeration-district data for Birmingham and ward data for the Conurbation as a whole. It is to be hoped that it will allow a wider range of participants – students of urban problems, policy makers, social workers, local and national government officers, regional planners and above all, the people of the region themselves – to take an active part in shaping the Conurbation's future.

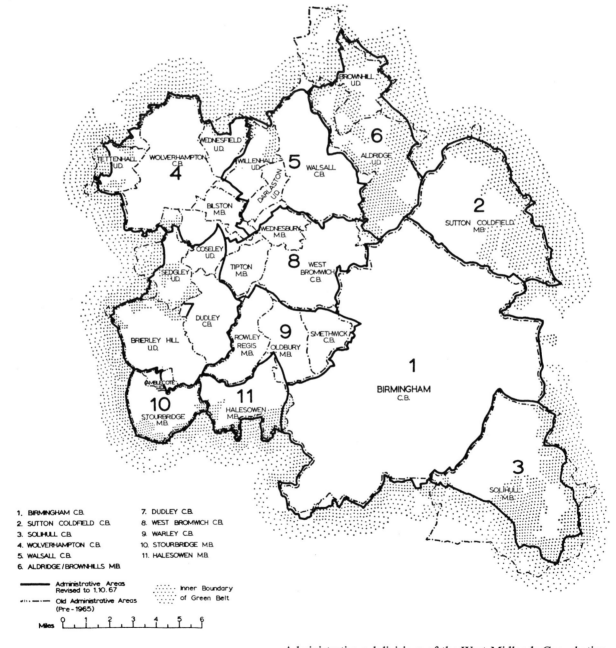

1. BIRMINGHAM C.B.
2. SUTTON COLDFIELD C.B.
3. SOLIHULL C.B.
4. WOLVERHAMPTON C.B.
5. WALSALL C.B.
6. ALDRIDGE/BROWNHILLS M.B.

7. DUDLEY C.B.
8. WEST BROMWICH C.B.
9. WARLEY C.B.
10. STOURBRIDGE M.B.
11. HALESOWEN M.B.

Administrative Areas
Revised to 1.10.67

Old Administrative Areas
(Pre - 1965)

Inner Boundary
of Green Belt

Miles 0 1 2 3 4 5 6

Administrative subdivisions of the West Midlands Conurbation

Character of a Conurbation

A computer atlas of Birmingham and the Black Country

Kenneth E Rosing BA PhD
Lecturer in Geography in the University of London
at King's College

Peter A Wood BSc PhD
Lecturer in Geography in the University of London
at University College

University of London Press Ltd

ISBN 0340 11879 2

University of London Press Ltd
St Paul's House Warwick Lane London EC4

Printed and bound in Great Britain by
Hazell Watson & Viney Ltd, Aylesbury, Bucks

Foreword

The Birmingham–Black Country Conurbation provides a classic example of the growth of an industrial concentration. The technical changes of the Industrial Revolution created new demands for the mineral resources that underlay South Staffordshire. The construction of canals and railways assisted the transformation of what had been a rather remote and sparsely populated upland area into a great focus of manufacturing industry. During the latter part of the eighteenth and in the nineteenth century, people were attracted in large numbers to work in the mines and factories. When the mines were exhausted or flooded out it was found possible to adapt the economic activities to new tasks. Specialization in metals remained important but more complex processes were undertaken. As the mines closed and blast furnaces were put out, the appearance of the Black Country began to change, the smoke began to lessen and the pit heaps and waste lands were colonized by green vegetation.

Standing away from the coalfield Birmingham drew in people to its metal transforming industries: it became also the commercial centre of the whole industrial region. Eventually it emerged as the regional capital of the West Midlands.

It is a story, with some notable exceptions, 'of industrial acceleration in which the needs of man took second place to the demands of manufacture'. In more recent times, as the Conurbation has continued to grow in population and in economic activity, the needs of individual men and women have become more central problems. Though many contributions have been made, the full story of efforts to improve housing conditions, to re-vegetate the derelict land, to provide better town layouts, to stimulate education and the social services has still to be told. A basic problem has been that of adapting a pattern of cities, developed to meet the industrial demands of a former age, to meet new concepts and standards of life. And to do this while still maintaining its impetus as a major industrial centre.

The authors of this Atlas rightly refer to the plans that have been laid since 1948 for an improved environment and to the thought now being given to ways of solving crucial problems such as those of housing and 'overspill'. More could be said of the achievements of post-war planning. Rightly, they stress the need for coordinated planning of a group of cities and towns that have grown together but for which a number of authorities share responsibility. There is little doubt that this Atlas, by revealing, on common bases, distribution patterns for the whole Conurbation, will contribute significantly to the understanding of the problems that we now face in continuing, indeed accelerating, efforts to provide a new environment for work, home, education and leisure. When maps are drawn setting out information in a geographical or spatial setting, new problems for enquiry are revealed. Taken together the maps provide us with a synoptic view of the social and economic geography of the area and enable the reader to make his own thoughtful appreciation of the problems of urban change and urban planning. The Atlas should be widely used in the West Midlands not only by town and country planners but by all who teach the need for an understanding of the geographical environment. For others it will be equally valuable as a well documented case study of a major industrial conurbation. The Atlas also brings to our attention the use that may be made of the computer for the rapid presentation of information in cartographic form. The authors are careful to explain the value and the limitations of the methods they employ and of the data they use. However, there is little doubt that the Atlas is a clear and effective demonstration of the increasingly valuable role that computer mapping has to play in the study of geographical conditions and in the application of geographical study to the improvement of the environment. The methods used in producing this Atlas will supplement, not replace, the older well-tried methods of study: in particular the need for careful field study of the character of the communities and places that together form the Conurbation will remain. The methods do, however, provide us with new tools which, if well used, can speed the process of presenting information on an areal basis. The maps indicate new questions for inquiry: they reveal the degree of challenge offered by problems of replacement and renewal, adaptation and rebuilding. The ability to make such maps should enable us, in the future, to plan more effectively. The maps prompt us to form our own view of the nature of the urban environment that we should seek to create.

Thus I welcome the production of the Atlas both as a timely and most encouraging experiment in the presentation and analysis of data and as an aid to the understanding of some important aspects of the social and economic geography of a great industrial region.

M. J. Wise

Preface

This atlas is very much the result of a chance coincidence of complementary interests. At the outset, one author was exploring the rather novel problems of computer mapping while the other contemplated the perennial difficulties of understanding the West Midlands Conurbation. The manner in which they came to appreciate the validity of each other's initial interest has been one of the most rewarding aspects of the work. During this process outside help has been of critical importance. First, the Centre for Urban and Regional Studies of the University of Birmingham allowed us to use its ward and enumeration-district data for the 1966 Sample Census. This made it possible to experiment with the mapping techniques and to explore the socio–economic fabric of the Conurbation. We are deeply grateful to Professor J. B. Cullingworth, Director of the Centre, for his help and for the stimulating discussions with his staff. Secondly, none of the maps could have been produced nor the technical problems overcome without the unstinting aid of the staff of the Computer Centre at University College London, under the direction of Professor Paul Samet. They have provided continuous encouragement in spite of what at times seemed to be impossible demands.

The two individuals whose pioneering interest in the possibilities of computer maps has provided the greatest stimulus to our work have been Professor Howard T. Fisher, of the Laboratory for Computer Graphics and Spatial Analysis at Harvard University, and Professor J. T. Coppock, of the Department of Geography, University of Edinburgh. The former helped particularly in obtaining a scholarship to enable one of the authors to gain technical training at Harvard, where the program was developed under a Ford Foundation grant. The latter pointed out the possibilities of census mapping in the West Midlands and, through his encouragement, kept the project alive in the face of difficulties.

Other technical help has come from the Cartography Units of the Departments of Geography at King's College, which produced the histograms, and at University College London, which drew the non-computer maps. Help in typing the various stages of the manuscript also came from the secretarial staff of the two departments. As always, we owe many thanks to the individuals concerned.

The atlas is primarily intended as a set of maps, whose patterns, with the accompanying statistics, may provide information which can be used by others for their own purposes. The commentaries are offered as a background explanation to set the maps in the context of the planning problems of both the Conurbation and the wider West Midlands region. In devising the written sections, help and advice has come from several individuals and organizations in the region. In particular the Director of the West Midlands Study, Mr John Stevenson, and his staff have been very encouraging. Only when the results of their crucially important work become available, will the information in the atlas take on its full value as an aid to planning. Similarly the observations of the staff of the West Midland Regional Office of the Ministry of Housing and Local Government and of local planning authorities in the Conurbation at an early stage of our work were of immense value. Finally, we must express our appreciation of the critical comments of Dr G. M. Lomas, then of the Department of Town and Country Planning, the University of Manchester, particularly in the discussions of housing problems in the region. In spite of all this help, we need hardly add that we take responsibility for all of the views expressed in the atlas.

Our principal hope in presenting this work is that all those in the region who are at present attempting to devise a coherent framework for its planning will find the atlas of some value, both for their own work and in communicating the needs of the Conurbation to a wider public.

K.E.R.

P.A.W.

Contents

Contents

Introductory maps and tables

Introduction
The Planning Context

In 1966 the West Midlands Conurbation housed an estimated 2·38 million people in an area of about twenty-five by twenty miles. Giant urbanized areas such as this are one of the most distinctive geographical expressions of modern industrialized society and the complexity of their problems produces intricate spatial patterns of human life within them. This atlas is an attempt to analyse these patterns for the West Midlands, using the most comprehensive and detailed information available, from the ten per cent sample census of 1966, and a system of computer mapping that allows such data to be displayed quickly and accurately. The maps, in effect, present a series of facets of the area in the mid 1960s although, because of the nature of the data, they do not present any information on changes through time. Many features of the urban and demographic structure of the Conurbation will be discussed in the commentaries associated with each pair of maps. This introduction sketches the general character of the Conurbation, highlighting the planning problems that it has posed during the past twenty years and will continue to pose in the future.

Form of the Conurbation
The Conurbation consists of two sections that are broadly distinct in their urban structures, to some extent in their economic activities and often in their social and political attitudes. In 1966, 1,067,000 of its people (41,000 less than 5 years earlier) lived in Birmingham, an urban area with all of the recognizable traits of a large metropolitan centre – in fact, the regional metropolis (Reference 12*) of the West Midlands (this region is officially defined to include the five counties of Staffordshire, Warwickshire, Worcestershire, Shropshire and Herefordshire, with a total population of 4,915,000). In form, the city is broadly concentric in layout, successive zones of past growth, with distinctive types of housing and road pattern, focusing on the well developed central business district (References 27, 28). Beyond its boundaries, to the north-east and south-east, Sutton Coldfield and Solihull form distinctive and rapidly growing communities, housing 179,000 people in 1966, which act primarily as commuter satellites of Birmingham. The rest of the Conurbation, fused on to the western side of the city, houses more people; 1,136,000 in 1966 (65,000 more than in 1961), and is popularly known as 'The Black Country'. This name has been inherited from the industrial character of the area during the height of its mid-nineteenth-century prosperity. Strictly speaking it traditionally applies neither to the large towns of Wolverhampton and Walsall nor to the more recent residential settlements on the periphery of the main industrial region. Nevertheless, in what follows the term 'Black Country' will be used to indicate the whole area of the built-up Conurbation to the west of Birmingham. The term embodies all of the qualities of the nineteenth-century 'con-urban' landscape – an amalgam of localities, some sizeable towns, some industrial villages, some simply rows of terraced houses or groups of factories, haphazardly arranged in a matrix of industrial sprawl, derelict land, railway lines and little used canals. 'The Character of the Conurbation' was the title given by the authors of *Conurbation*, a classic work on the West Midlands published in 1948 (Reference 30, pp. 18–25), to a series of evocative photographs that set the scene of their study. In our preoccupation with a statistical

*See Appendix II, p. 126.

analysis of the Conurbation's character, the physical images presented there should not be forgotten. Since *Conurbation* was produced, modern elements have been added to the landscape, rebuilding some of the old areas, filling in the gaps and expanding its periphery with houses, factories and roads. Unfortunately no new order has arisen from the inherited chaos in spite of the possibilities for improvement that were suggested by that pioneering study.

Problems of planning the Conurbation
The idea of a 'conurbation' as a recognizable type of human settlement, gigantic in scale and complex in structure, is not new. The word itself is attributed to Patrick Geddes (Reference 10) who saw in 1915 repeated examples in the industrialized world of urban communities that had merged together during the nineteenth century and so presented huge problems of planning. By the early years of this century the merging had progressed in both a physical sense, giving landscapes of more or less continuous urban and industrial development, and also functionally, with the constituent parts becoming increasingly dependent upon each other for the provision of housing, services and employment. The main concern of the pioneer planners of that time was to remove the physically repellent environment of the conurbations. In recent decades, however, the attention of planners has been diverted more towards the functional aspects of urban development. The concept of the city region, for example, has become very fashionable, embracing rural areas and satellite towns under the influence of cities but outside their built-up areas. This idea has already made a permanent mark upon regional and transport planning and upon proposals for administrative reform in Britain. There is no doubt that concepts of functional unity are of fundamental importance today in understanding the task of planning but the physical problems of the built-up areas of our conurbations still present the most urgent challenge to the social effectiveness of planning; how can progress be made towards a humane and civilized physical and social environment for their millions of inhabitants? It is arguable that the inability to make any real headway in solving the problems of general physical renewal, catalogued twenty years ago by *Conurbation*, is the clearest sign of failure. The planners' new-found preoccupation with city regions might be regarded cynically as a shirking of that challenge.

To be fair, post-war experience in the West Midlands, if nothing else, has demonstrated that the Conurbation's problems cannot be divorced from those of the surrounding region. It has also shown that the situation within large urban areas is prone to change very rapidly, possibly outdating any solutions even before they have had time to be implemented. A passage from *Conurbation* (page 27) illustrates this dilemma:

> The [West Midland] Group is of the opinion that by the reclamation of wasteland, by the preservation of unspoiled land and by the restoration of misused land, the Conurbation could become a more attractive and efficient place. There is room in the area for present industries to expand naturally; there is room for its inhabitants to be decently housed, there is room for the preservation of those natural amenities so necessary for a population closely occupied in industry. There is room for everything that is needful but there is no room to waste and in economic and imaginative planning no authority can afford to ignore its neighbour.

Introduction

There is no doubt that in 1948 this study represented a degree of vision and skill in facing the problems of the West Midlands Conurbation that sadly has been unequalled since. Unfortunately, its fundamental propositions as stated here have largely been proved false. Shortage of space for housing and industry has been acute. Open land and derelict land alike have been built on almost to the limit so that the open areas that were characteristic of the Black Country even during the most notorious period of its history have disappeared under the now continuous urban sprawl. Even today, regional planners are proposing to continue this process by 'scraping up' whatever land remains available for house building (Reference 5, paragraph 136).

Even if the calculations of demand for the limited available land in *Conurbation* were mistaken, its warning about the need for cooperation in planning the Black Country was prophetic. Virtually no act of coordinated planning took place within the Conurbation at least until the late 1950s, when some co-operation in outlining strategic road developments was begun. Even the policy for the overspill of population, which by definition must cut across administrative boundaries, was promulgated until 1965 by a joint consultative committee of the three county authorities and Birmingham, with no representation from the Black Country county boroughs. Thus, although many of the current difficulties of the Conurbation are attributable to population growth in the 1950s and 1960s, the rise of private and commercial motor traffic, the expansion of service employment and higher living standards, in addition the machinery for planning has proved deficient in its lack of preparation for these changes.

Framework for post-war planning

Since 1948, planning in the West Midlands region as a whole has proceeded on the basis of the *West Midlands Plan* (Reference 1), prepared for the Ministry of Town and Country Planning by Abercrombie and Jackson. This sought a logical and practical solution to the problems generated by the Conurbation and even today it is in the regional context that any ultimate solution must be set. The Plan set a ceiling population for the conurbation of 2,176,000 by 1962, within physical limits to be defined by a proposed Green Belt. This 'containment' policy has been implemented with some modifications in response to the growing pressures for land, especially from Birmingham in the 1960s. In spite of never achieving full statutory status, the Green Belt remains the most successful example of a regional-scale policy in the West Midlands. It is significant that it is a restrictive policy and has been maintained at the insistence of the surrounding county councils against pressures from local authorities within the Conurbation. These pressures against the Green Belt have become more intense in recent years, mainly because of the neglect of effective positive planning measures to complement it. *The West Midlands Plan* expected that the population of the Conurbation would grow to 2,428,000 by 1962 and therefore emphasized the need for an active *overspill* policy to transfer 252,000 people to planned communities beyond the Green Belt. In fact, in spite of a higher rate of natural increase and immigration than the *West Midlands Plan* expected, the population of the Conurbation in 1962 was 50,000 less than its prediction (Reference 7, p. 43). A large number of people must therefore have left the Conurbation to live in the surrounding areas and, since only 25,000

moved under planned overspill schemes between 1945 and 1965, most of this migration was voluntary.

Abercrombie and Jackson had some inkling of what was required and were certainly more realistic about the likely situation than *Conurbation* (Reference 7, p. 42). They hoped that the proper planning of self-contained overspill communities, with their own local employment, would prevent the further development of commuting from and across the Green Belt into the Conurbation. Unfortunately, another symptom of the failure of planning in spite of earlier warnings was the rapid growth of long-distance journeys to work to the Conurbation in the 1950s. Between 1951 and 1961, the numbers of commuters from Green Belt areas into Birmingham and the older parts of the Black Country almost doubled, growing by 25,670 to 56,620. Meanwhile, the 'newer conurbation' areas (including Sutton Coldfield, Solihull, Aldridge, Wednesfield, Tettenhall, Sedgeley and Halesowen) contributed 34,580 more commuters to these areas, a total by 1961 of 94,380 (Reference 19, Ch. 2).

Current planning organization

We have now described, in very broad outline, the recent history of planning the West Midlands Conurbation – the efforts that have been made to control its unruly growth with inadequate means. Renewed efforts at coordinated planning on a regional scale have been made in Britain in recent years, most particularly through the setting up in early 1965 of advisory Regional Economic Planning Councils. These consist of representatives of regional interests and expertise and are supported by Economic Planning Boards formed by groups of technical and administrative officers from a variety of ministry backgrounds. In the West Midlands, two studies of the region's planning problems have so far (late 1969) resulted from this new structure. The first, *The West Midlands: A Regional Study* (Reference 5) although begun earlier, was produced by the Department of Economic Affairs in 1965. Following this, the First Report of the West Midlands Economic Planning Council was published in 1967 (Reference 29). Entitled *The West Midlands: Patterns of Growth*, it summarized the views of the local advisory body on the D.E.A.'s proposals for the region. These two documents represent official attitudes to planning priorities in the region up to 1981. A study which analysed trends since 1948 in considerable detail and produced its own estimates of future population change and housing and employment needs in the region was *Population Growth and Planning Policy*, published in 1965 by the West Midlands Social and Political Research Unit of the University of Birmingham (Reference 7). A good deal of new research effort has been stimulated by the new-found interest in regional planning in the West Midlands but these three documents, together with another written in 1967 and published in 1970 (Reference 19), provide the basis for the current appreciation of future planning problems in the region.

The future overspill problem – the demand for housing

The size of the overspill problem in the West Midlands is central to its planning, both because it represents the limited self-sufficiency of the Conurbation in stark statistical terms and because it indicates how this will impinge upon the surrounding areas. Essentially, the problem is one of supplying houses for a demand that is growing rapidly in response to a number of developments. These can be summarized into three main groups:

1 *The growth in the numbers of families needing individual dwellings*

Two elements should be distinguished, each with their own problems of estimation; a) population growth and b) changing housing standards.

a) Estimates of population growth require the calculation of future birth and death rates for the resident population, rates of migration into and out of the area and the likely growth of the immigrant population once in residence. Such estimates are bound to be very tentative and subject to constant revision. Birth rates, after increasing up to the mid-1960s, have more recently declined, but we cannot tell how far this decline will continue. Greater longevity, with more retired people in the population, is an important trend at the other end of the age range. Migration forecasting is very difficult. 'Unpredictable' events, such as the Commonwealth Immigrants Act of 1962 or future progress in government aid to the development areas of the north and west of the country may be crucially important in their effect upon migration to the region.

b) Changing standards of housing in the future are reflected most simply in the declining average size of households. *The West Midlands Study* suggested indirectly that this would fall for the region from 3·11 persons per household in 1961 to 2·88 by 1981. *Population Growth and Planning Policy*, however, thought that a more likely figure by 1981 would be 2·81 (Reference 7, page 26). This difference would increase the demand for houses by only 26,000 but it may have wider implications in terms of 'household fission'. This term implies the impact upon housing demand of social changes such as earlier marriage, smaller families, less sharing of parent's dwellings by single persons and young married couples and of relatives' houses by retired people. As living standards rise these processes, whereby families now living in the same household come to expect to live separately, will have an increasing impact (see variable 8).

Estimates in the *West Midlands Study* for the period between 1963 and 1981 suggested that the number of new houses required to accomodate this local growth in demand, through both population growth and higher housing standards, would be around 148,000 in the Conurbation. The First Report of the Regional Planning Council (Reference 29) added 30,000 dwellings to the regional figure to allow for net immigration, half of them in the Conurbation.

2 *The need to replace obsolete housing*

In the post-war plans, the slums of the Conurbation provided the crucial social and political stimulus to planning in the West Midlands. In spite of progress in slum clearance since then (Reference 28), the First Report of the Regional Planning Council pointed out that the size of the problem is as great as ever. The creation of slums is a continuous process and the *West Midlands Study* estimated that 250,000 new houses for the region would be needed by 1981 to replace the worst sub-standard dwellings, 130,000 of them in the Conurbation. Even if these are built, the Planning Council pointed out that by then there would still be 120,000 houses in the region older than 100 years and another 400,000 of between 65 and 100 years old (Reference 30, para 85).

3 *The need to reduce overcrowding in the existing housing stock*

This problem is acute in the Conurbation, particularly in areas that have received large numbers of immigrants in recent years. It may well be larger than envisaged by the *West Midlands Study* in 1965, which indicated that 62,000 houses would be needed by 1981 to relieve overcrowding in the Conurbation. Nevertheless, this figure was agreed both by the First Report of the Planning Council and by *Population Growth and Planning Policy*.

Table 1 summarizes the situation described above, presenting the figures in the *West Midlands Study* (page 41) which were endorsed by the First Report (page 21) of the Regional Planning Council except where it added a figure of 30,000 to allow for migration into the region. The regional figure is also indicated to show the scale of the Conurbation's contribution to its problem.

Table 1
The need for houses 1963–81 number of dwellings in thousands

	1 New household formation	2 Replacement	3 Overcrowding	Total
Conurbation	148 (163)	130	62	340 (355)
Region	275 (305)	250	75	600 (630)
Source	*West Midlands Study* Table IX First report of the West Midlands Regional Economic Planning Council, page 21			

Population Growth and Planning Policy produced independent estimates for the 25 years from 1961 to 1986 which add some detail to this picture, especially separating the needs of Birmingham from the rest of the Conurbation and pinpointing the position of the 'Conurbation fringe' – the Green Belt zone.

Table 2
The need for houses 1961–86 number of dwellings in thousands

	1 New household formation			2 Replacement	3 Overcrowding	Total
	Natural increase	Household fission	Immigration			
Birmingham	96	34		81	30	241
Rest of conurbation	81	57		67	25	230
Total	*117*	*91*	*33*	*148*	*55*	*471*
Conurbation fringe	50	35		17	5	107
Region	374	227	60	250	107	988
Source	*Population Growth and Planning Policy* Table X, page 34					

The difference between the calculation in Table 1 of 600,000 houses for the region between 1963 and 1981 and the 988,000 needed between 1961 and 1986 in Table 2 is mainly accounted for by the differing time periods. 79,000 houses were built between 1961 and 1964 and a further 210,000 are likely to be needed between 1981 and 1986. The latter high figure will result from the children of the post-war 'bulge' generation getting married and setting up home. In addition, *Population Growth and Planning Policy* allowed 60,000 houses for its estimate of net immigration and 26,000 to allow for extra household fission by 1986 (page 36).

Introduction

Thus the two estimates are quite close if these adjustments are taken into account. It is agreed by all authorities that the Conurbation will need to accommodate as many extra households by 1981 as already existed in the whole of the city of Birmingham in 1966. The number will also continue to increase substantially after that date. In practical terms this implies the building of 26,000 houses per year up to 1986 for the Conurbation and its periphery. Between 1961 and 1964, about 18,700 were built per year in and around the Conurbation. This represents a considerable shortfall, although the regional rate of building has increased since 1964 from 31,000 to over 40,000 houses per year.

The future overspill problem – the supply of land

The Regional Study was not worried about the capacity to build this amount of housing, at least within the period up to 1981 with which it was concerned. It saw the key problem as one of where to locate these houses – where to find the land on which to build them? It is the answer to this question that determines the need for population overspill. Of prime importance is the capacity of the Conurbation to take more housing. The *West Midlands Study* confirmed that there is no reasonable prospect of decently accommodating even the natural increase of the Conurbation by 1981 within its present area (para 195). In fact, if its pressing needs of urban renewal are to be satisfied, its population, especially in the Birmingham half, will have to be reduced. The Study suggested a population of about 2,235,000 by 1981, with Birmingham declining perhaps by 200,000 to just over 900,000, while the rest of the Conurbation may rise by about 50,000, (para 232). The contribution of the Conurbation to the 600,000 houses needed in the region by 1981 was suggested to be about 170,000; 75,000 through redevelopment, 65,000 on open land already earmarked under existing development plans for housing and a further 30,000 which the Study hoped might be 'scraped up', 'by various devices' (paragraph 136). This suggestion sounds alarmingly like a last despairing attempt to shoehorn people into a scatter of small unsuitable plots of land without regard to any long-term planning aims. After 1981 there will apparently be no land left in the Conurbation except from the redevelopment of existing built-up areas. The shortage of land in the Conurbation to satisfy its demand for 340,000 houses up to this date will be equivalent to 170,000 dwellings which will have to be provided by some form of overspill, whether planned or voluntary. The First Report of the Economic Planning Council accepted these estimates, although it urged that a more detailed study of land availability in the Conurbation should be carried out, and added 15,000 houses to the demand side for the immigration that it expected. The contribution of the Chelmsley Wood incursion into the Green Belt to the east of Birmingham, approved in 1964, reduces the figure by about 20,000, to give a final demand for overspill of 165,000 houses, about 530,000 people. Other such incursions, in Worcestershire ('The South-West Sector') are now being urged as planners begin to suspect the practicability of massive long-range overspill. The First Report, like the Regional Study before it, emphasized the unprecedented scale of the movements that they proposed and particularly their significance for a much more active policy than in the past of employment decentralization from the Conurbation. Otherwise, the growth of long-distance commuting and the strain on the already overstretched transportation network of the Conurbation region will become increasingly acute.

The Regional Council presented the following table to indicate where the houses might be located. It is beyond the scope of this commentary to discuss these proposals in detail. Some, like the new towns at Redditch and Telford (Dawley–Wellington–Oakengates) are going ahead while others are no more than paper proposals.

Table 3

Proposed overspill schemes 1963–81		Population intake 1963–81 *thousands*
Town development schemes		
a Previously agreed	Daventry	22
	Droitwich	13
	other	19
b Under discussion	Tamworth, Stafford and Lichfield	50
New towns		
	Redditch	35
	Dawley	50
Possible new developments		
Expansion of Dawley–Wellington–Oakengates		50
	Worcester	25
	Burton upon Trent	40
	North Staffordshire	50
	South-West Sector	50
Expansion around the Green Belt for overspill purposes		150
Total		*554*
Source	First report of the West Midlands Economic Planning Council, pagagraph 225	

The character of a conurbation

In conclusion, the foreseeable patterns of future change in the Conurbation may be seen as the continuation of a long-established pattern; the 'flight to the fringes', a decentralizing of population from the older built-up areas into the newer, more spacious periphery. While examining the maps in this atlas in their planning context, it may be helpful to think of two contrasting types of area within the Conurbation, augmented by a third intermediate category, which overlie the division already established between the Birmingham and Black Country halves.

First, the *older areas* of predominantly nineteenth-century housing, much in an unsatisfactory condition as the information displayed later will confirm. In Birmingham these consist of the inner suburbs of the city, while in the Black Country areas of this type both cluster around the centres of the towns and form many distinct industrial villages. These communities still generate intense local feeling, based upon long-established social ties and industrial specializations within the undifferentiated sprawl of the Conurbation. Nevertheless, they are areas of marked emigration, with planned redevelopment projects taking their toll (normally only about one half of the original numbers can be housed in a rebuilt slum area). Higher earning power, especially among younger families, also prompts a voluntary search for more pleasant living environments.

These more pleasant conditions are found in the second type of area, the *newer conurbation*, where house building has been proceeding rapidly during the past 20 years. Some of the outer areas of Birmingham are included in this category but as the city has exhausted its supply of building land its inhabitants have tended to move to the nearby satellite towns of Solihull and Sutton Coldfield. Similarly, other areas around the Conurbation, such as Aldridge, and Wednesfield in the north, Sedgley and Tettenhall to the west and Halesowen and Stourbridge on the south may be categorized as 'newer conurbation' areas. Defined by their pre-1965 administrative divisions these gained 100,000 persons by net immigration between 1951 and 1963, giving a total growth of 128,000 over a population at the beginning of the period of 233,000 (Reference 7, page 7). In contrast the older conurbation, including Birmingham, lost 123,000 by migration during this period (80,000 from Birmingham), to give a total growth of only 27,000 for a 1951 population of 2·2 millions. The net loss by the whole Conurbation of 23,000 people through migration suggested by these figures must be explained in a wider geographical context. The fastest growing areas of the West Midlands Region outside the Conurbation are nearby, in the Green Belt. The population of this zone increased by 86,000 migrants between 1951 and 1963, so that the greater conurbation region had a final net increase by migration of about 60,000.

Thirdly, on a more detailed inspection of the Conurbation an *intermediate area* needs to be emphasized, even though it cannot be defined and examined statistically by administrative areas (in fact, the boundary changes of 1965 now make impossible even the above crude comparisons between the older and newer conurbation). This zone predominantly contains housing built between the two world wars and may be thought of as 'average' in its characteristics. It is occupied largely by a middle-aged middle class. The significance of this category, when compared with the problem areas of the older conurbation or the more spectacularly growing parts of the newer conurbation, can probably only be appreciated through a study of the type of maps that this atlas is designed to provide.

Viewing these three categories of area in their dynamic relationships with each other once more emphasizes the crux of the Conurbation's planning problems. The 'flight to the fringe' is being projected further, beyond the boundaries of the Conurbation as its remaining land, even in the newer areas, becomes occupied. As the Conurbation continues to grow the pressure for population increase and housing is now clearly on the Green Belt areas.

The Technical Background

This study was originally conceived as a large-scale experiment in the application of the technique of computer mapping. Later, when satisfactory results began to be obtained, the project changed to become a study in the quantitative spatial description of the West Midlands Conurbation. This is as it should be – computer mapping, like all techniques, should not be regarded as an end in itself. There is nothing particularly desirable about producing maps on a computer and the only justification for this, or any technique, is that it increases the understanding of the phenomena being investigated.

It is hoped that in this atlas both the original and later objectives have, at least to a limited extent, been achieved. The technique has been uniformly applied in the study of a wide range of variables, despite formidable difficulties, and perhaps some new knowledge has been gained about the spatial aspects of the multivariate character of the Conurbation.

Recently there has been a marked quickening of interest in computer mapping among geographers and planners for two main reasons. First, the increasing size and power of computers and the sophistication of operating systems have made possible economic application of the technology. Secondly geographers, planners and others interested in spatial phenomena have become more aware that most conventional statistical techniques do not adequately deal with the spatial aspects of their problems. The study of space and the phenomena that are distributed in that space is central to geography and in this particular context indispensable to planning.

Computer mapping

Four types of maps are commonly drawn by computer; the isopleth map, the choropleth map, the Thiessen polygon map and the dot or graphic symbol map. Of these four, the first three can be drawn by the SYMAP system 5·12 (SYMAP was developed by the Laboratory for Computer Graphics and Spatial Analysis, Graduate School of Design, Harvard University, Cambridge, Massachusetts, under the directorship of H. T. Fisher with the assistance of a Ford Foundation research and development grant). The isopleth portion of SYMAP version 5·12 (modified by K. Rosing) was used for the production of all the computer maps in this book. SYMAP is only one of a number of systems for the production of computer maps. It is, however, fully operational, widely available and probably the best known of such systems.

Several types of information must be given to the computer for it to make a map. Obviously these include details of the type of map, the scale, and the method of portraying the information. The main problems, however, concern the specification of the outline of the map, the position of the data points within this outline and the quantities that can be attributed to the points. The locations of points, whether part of the boundary or individual data points, are described by supplying their north–south and east–west coordinate 'addresses' on a grid, such as the National Grid. In the case of the boundary lines, the locations of their major points of inflexion, supplied in consecutive order, are sufficient to give a more or less generalized outline.

Several limitations are imposed by the technique of isopleth mapping. The variables must be applied at points rather than to areas and the values must be interval or ratio in their class of measurement. The data upon which this study is based is the 1966 ten per cent Sample Census, using enumeration districts in Birmingham and census wards for the maps of the Conurbation. It was made available in machine readable form through the courtesy of the Centre for Urban and Regional Studies of the University of Birmingham. This data refers to districts rather than points, so that each district must be represented by a centroid, defined as the centre of the largest inscribed circle – the point most remote from the borders of the data zone. In a few cases where large open areas were included within the district (e.g. around Sutton Park), the point was adjusted to a position which more closely reflects the population distribution. We have assumed in using these points that they are an areal average at which the variable's mathematical average for each area is applied. This is of course not 'true' but, in the same way as the value for an area represents the mean condition of that variable rather than a 'true' value, the central point, as a mean spatial point, extends this reasoning. In addition the generalization inherent in isopleth mapping prevents serious violation of the assumption.

An isopleth map is constructed by passing lines through points of estimated equal value. The estimate is calculated on the basis of the information that is available on a grid of either regularly or irregularly spaced known points. Values for unknown points are interpolated on the basis of a consistent mathematical criterion. Any of a number of algorithms might have been used; see for example C. F. Schmid (Reference 40) or more recently V. Conrad (Reference 33), but SYMAP interpolates or extrapolates in the following manner. (This description of the SYMAP algorithm is, necessarily, generalized: for exact details see Shepard, Reference 41.) A grid of cells of a specified size is imposed by the computer upon the map which is to be created. The cells are generally the size and shape of a single printing character in the line printer of the computer, in this case $\frac{1}{8}$ inch high by $\frac{1}{10}$ inch wide. As the scale of the desired map is altered the proportion of the map contained within each cell increases or decreases. Certain cells contain the real spatial location of the known data points which are then printed in the appropriate class shading. The values of all other cells must be interpolated (or extrapolated). The calculation is made on the basis of the nearest four to ten known cells, the exact number depending upon their density and distribution. The values in each of the selected known cells are weighted in proportion to the inverse square of the straight line distance from the unknown cell ($1/d^2$). The weighted values are then adjusted on the basis of the spatial distribution of the known cells and to allow for the local trend of the surface. The adjusted weighted values are then averaged and the resultant value is assigned to the appropriate unknown cell. This may be done for every cell in the map but to save time it is generally repeated for every third cell horizontally and every second cell vertically. The intervening cells are then filled in by simple arithmetic interpolation. The resultant number field, thought of as a continuous surface, has the desirable qualities of containing no folds, creases or tears, passes through all points of known value and is mathematically consistent. It may be considered as a 'most probable' surface based on the given information and certain mathematical constraints. At the point of printing, the values in the cells are replaced by appropriate printing symbols. The isopleth is then defined as the junction between two areas of symbols which represent particular adjacent ranges of values.

The Sample Census

There are several difficulties with the ten per cent Sample Census data, especially in dealing with small areas. It was nevertheless used as the most up-to-date and comprehensive source of detailed information available. The 1961 census material was felt to be too dated, even though some information was available from the 100 per cent enumeration. The next census will be in 1971 and much of its material will not be available until one or two years later. Also, many of the indices will be coded and calculated again only on the basis of a ten per cent sample. For these reasons it was not felt to be desirable to either postpone the mapping or to use less current data.

A comprehensive assessment of the sampling procedure used in 1966, on the basis of a post-census check is not yet available. A report on this subject will be contained in the final statistical assessment of the Census. A preliminary discussion is available in any of the published reports of county statistics (Reference 11). In 1966, the ten per cent sample was taken on the basis of a sampling frame estimated from the 1961 lists of dwellings and large non-private residential establishments. Several sources were consulted to correct and update these lists and ten per cent of the defined dwellings were visited. Inaccuracies in sampling have placed doubt on the confidence with which expansion of the sample to the full population can be carried out for comparisons with past censuses. This problem is not important in this study since intercensal comparisons are not directly considered.

A more serious problem arises in the use of the sample for small units. The smaller the sampled population the lower must be the confidence in its representativeness. This is not a significant consideration in any of the 161 wards used in mapping the whole of the Conurbation, the smallest of which has a population of 4,540 persons (mean of 14,733, standard deviation (SD) of 7,642) and 170 dwellings (mean of 4,630, SD 2,280). Of the 472 census enumeration districts used to produce the maps of Birmingham, the smallest contained no persons (mean 2,359, SD of 590) and no dwellings (mean 721, SD of 188). These resulted from anomalous boundary conditions and were edited out of the data tape. The tape was also found to contain twelve enumeration districts with less than 170 persons. These were aggregated with contiguous districts, in each case to make the resulting areas as compact as possible. After this aggregation none of the 451 remaining enumeration districts contained less than 290 persons. (Throughout this volume the terms persons, households, dwellings, etc., refer to the estimated total number obtained by multiplying the sample by ten.)

123 ratio or percentage variables were derived from the simple enumerations printed on the district data sheets. By inspection this was reduced to 60, variables being eliminated if they were duplicated by others or if they appeared to be of no particular interest. This process was carried out to lessen the chance that a particular type of datum in the census might be ignored. The chosen variables were checked for suspicious values and their frequency distributions were examined by the construction of histograms (program by K. Rosing). Any obvious errors in the data tapes were then rectified.

Factor analysis

The two sixty-variable matrices (one for Birmingham and one for the Conurbation) were then subjected to factor analysis.

IBM Scientific Subroutine FACTO (modified by K. Rosing) was used for this analysis (Reference 36). The rationale of factor analysis is quite simple (King, Reference 38, or for more detail Harman, Reference 35, Murdie, Reference 21). Basically it is a method of grouping. It may be used to either group variables (R mode) or areas (Q mode). Given a raw-data matrix some number of variables wide, each represented as a column, by some number of areas long, each represented by a row, then every bit of information will occur in some cell of the matrix. R-mode factor analysis attempts to group the variables by searching for order in the variation within each of the columns. Q-mode attempts to group areas by searching for order in the variation within each of the rows. In this study R-mode factor analysis has been used. The first assumption in factor analysis is that there is some composite structure of relationships, in a scalar manner, in the real world. The next assumption is that no individual variable can measure this structure adquately, although each measures some facet of it better than any other. First the zero-order correlations between all variables are calculated and the interrelationships of these correlations are then examined. A small number of uncorrelated common factors are arrived at which account for a high percentage of the total variation in the zero-order correlation matrix. The principle of 'simple structure' dictates that, in so far as is possible, each original variable is highly correlated with one factor and minimally correlated with all others. This is the orthogonal solution; other solutions allow oblique factors which are then intercorrelated themselves. There are many difficulties in the interpretation of factor analysis; these include such problems as the indeterminancy and the instability of the solution. For a discussion of these problems see Harman (Reference 35). At this point factor analysis was used to eliminate a certain amount of duplication or redundancy in the data and to identify a smaller number of variables which still covered the full range of major factors. The final matrix for analysis was composed of thirty-two variables which were in the same factors in the five-factor solution of both areas. These thirty-two were not the variables which were most interrelated. Rather they were variables which were most closely identified with the different factors when more factors were generated (nine and thirteen). Thus variables which were basically measuring the same variation were largely excluded from the matrix. In addition ten variables which were identified with different factors in the two (Birmingham and Conurbation) matrices or which had relatively low relationships with the factors were included after inspection indicated that they were probably measuring important characteristics not otherwise present.

The factor analysis was then repeated for the two forty-two-variable matrices. The results were used for five purposes. First, from the remaining forty-two variables the twenty-two presented in this volume were selected. Second, the organization of the variables presented in this volume into five sections reflects the five factors. Third, the interrelationships between variables, as evidenced by the factor analysis, were used in writing the interpretive text. Fourth, the maps introducing each section were calculated from the coefficients given in the factor structure. Fifth, these maps were used in the final identification of the factors and in the interpretive text.

The eigenvalues and their cumulative percentages are presented in Table 4. A summary table of the factor loadings

Introduction

and the communalities of variables is presented at the beginning of each section in the discussion accompanying each factor map. Factor loadings can be interpreted as the simple correlation between each variable and the specified factor. Communalities indicate the degree of interrelationship of that variable with the full matrix of simple correlations.

Table 4

Conurbation	Factors 1	2	3	4	5
Eigenvalue	12·49	8·30	5·80	2·69	2·16
Cumulative percent of eigenvalues	29·74	49·51	63·51	69·72	74·87
Birmingham					
Eigenvalue	10·44	6·65	3·51	3·25	2·67
Cumulative percent of eigenvalues	24·86	40·70	49·05	56·78	63·13

Multiple correlation

Various aspects of the phenomena were also investigated using stepwise multiple regression and an analysis of certain partial correlations was carried out. IBM Scientific Subroutine Sample Program STEPR (modified by K. Rosing) was used for this analysis (Reference 36). For the multiple-regression and multiple-correlation analysis of certain dependent variables some independent variables had to be eliminated to correct for multicollinearity (King, Reference 38). The results of the stepwise multiple-correlation analysis appears in tabular form in the analysis of each variable (see Blalock, Reference 32, and Ezekiel, Reference 34, for meaning and interpretation of multiple correlation and regression).

The simple and multiple correlations tabulated are all significant at the 0·001 level of probability. The minimum simple correlation shown in the tables is determined by:

1 the general strength of correlation for the dependent variables
2 the interest of the correlation
3 considerations of the space available

The maximum stepwise multiple correlation is determined by:

1 the statistical significance of the partial correlation coefficients entering the equation
2 the interest and statistical significance of following simple correlations

Presentation of the maps

Several methods of dividing the data into classes for mapping were investigated and the particular problems of each choice were identified. The form of the statistical distribution and the range of the various variables differed widely. For this reason it was judged impossible to use standard break-points on all the maps. If standard break-points had been possible inter-map comparisons would have been rendered relatively easy. Conversely, if for each map the values had been ordered and divided into classes with an equal number of occurrences in each class, the readability of the maps would have been good but comparisons between maps would have been difficult. Division of the range of each variable into classes with equal sizes was used as the best compromise. Eight categories were

used for several reasons: other work in recent years has used such octile division of data (Atlas of London, Reference 37) and inter-city comparisons might thus be made possible; eight categories have been suggested as a general maximum for the eye to comprehend easily (Robinson, Reference 39); and finally the available range of characters on the computer line-printer prevent the representation of more than eight easily distinguishable shading categories, particularly as the original was reduced by a factor of three for publication.

A standard range and the octiles of that range were defined on the basis of the histogram of each variable. The histograms are presented in the interpretive text on each variable. Isolated extreme values were excluded at each end of the range if necessary. The range between the chosen maximum and minimum was then divided into eight equal intervals; each of these are represented on the map by different tone shading.

The maps should be read in a manner similar to a contour map, the lines defined by the junction of two areas of shading being interpreted as similar to a contour line. One important difference should be emphasized. Since a contour line accurately passes through points of *known* equal value, reliance may be placed upon its exact position. The isopleth on these maps passes through points of *inferred* equal value and as such is an average or general statement only. Isopleths deviate from the 'real' isometric line of the phenomena (if such could exist) but are the average or best estimate of its location. It is implicit that proceeding from the highest value class to the lowest value class entails passing through all intermediate value classes. A single high value in an area of low values will therefore cause a number of concentric rings of all the intermediate values to appear around it. These maps can be considered as the theoretically most probable isotropic surface representing each variable. However, high reliability should only be placed upon the broader regional patterns. Difficulties in the sample (see above) may cause the appearance of individually anomalous high or low values. Indeed the production of maps and consequent identification of such difficulties is perhaps a worthwhile exercise in itself.

In preparing each map for publication an overlay containing the main road pattern and the outline of the administrative area was prepared. The density of road pattern displayed was chosen to be sufficient for identification and comparison and yet not so dense as to inhibit the general 'look' of the map or to encourage too detailed small-area analysis.

Forty-nine maps are presented in this volume. With the exception of the first map of each section (a total of 5 maps) they portray the spatial distribution of each of twenty-two variables. For each variable the left-hand page shows the spatial distribution of the variable in the Conurbation of a scale of 1:190,000 (c. 1 inch to 3 miles), based on its 161 census wards. The right-hand page presents the same variable mapped for the city of Birmingham on a scale of 1:106,000 (c. 1 inch to 1·7 miles), based on the 472 (451 used in the actual mapping) enumeration districts in the city. Because of the statistical distribution of the variables (sometimes near normal and sometimes highly skewed) the extreme categories may contain relatively few observations. The standard octile range allows comparability, the same shading on each map representing the same portion of the variable in relation to the total range of the various indices. The full detail of the octile categorization has been retained in all maps to allow more detailed analysis; for a general analysis, however, it may be found most useful to follow the general trend of categories.

An introduction to each section is presented, together with a commentary on each pair of maps which attempts to bring together information derived from the statistical analyses, a comparison of the maps and a general knowledge of the Conurbation's problems. The commentaries deal with the definition of and qualifications attached to each variable, as well as its relevance and situation with respect to others. Data on the statistical distributions of each variable, on the factor analysis, the multiple-correlation and the simple-correlation analyses are presented in the hope that readers examining the spatial patterns will be enabled to develop interpretations that are relevant to their own interests. The final section of this Introduction, which now follows, summarizes the main practical points to be kept in mind when examining the maps.

Guide to the Use of the Atlas

Data

A wide range of census indices, or 'variables', as we have called them, are examined in this atlas. They were derived from special tabulations of the 1966 Sample Census, obtained from the General Register Office. Two maps have been prepared for each variable and were also prepared for all of the indices listed in Appendix I:

a) A map of the whole West Midlands Conurbation based upon data for its 161 electoral wards. These show broadly regional patterns of distribution for each variable.

b) A map of Birmingham (which, of course, also forms part of the area of the Conurbation maps) based upon data for the 472 census enumeration districts in the city. Much more detailed local patterns can be traced with this data.

The scope of any study based upon a census is inevitably limited by the types of data that it sets out to collect. Censuses are intended to delineate, in statistical terms, the ways in which people live and in Britain they do so by asking two main types of question. The first of these concerns the socio-economic structure of the population itself: age and sex characteristics, family size, employment types, skills and professions, migration and, more recently, car ownership, travel habits and levels of education. These data are normally expressed in terms of either individuals or of *household* units and families (see census definitions on page 21). The second type of question in the censuses concerns the type and quality of dwellings that are occupied by households; their size (usually in terms of the numbers of rooms), the type of tenure, the availability of certain basic amenities (w.c.s, baths, hot and cold water, sink and stove) and whether these are shared. The basic unit of measurement for these physical attributes of living is the *dwelling* although, since the adequacy of housing can only be judged in terms of its occupancy rate, many of the dwelling indices are related to household size and structure.

Organization of the sections

In this analysis of the 1966 Sample Census factor analysis is used to group together ranges of these population and housing variables that appear to be distinctively associated in their statistical variation (see Appendix I for a full list of these variables). Not surprisingly, measures of dwelling characteristics are very important in distinguishing between different types of area in the Conurbation; the physical equipment inherited from some two hundred years of growth, as has already been suggested in the Introduction, provides a crucial framework for understanding the Conurbation's problems. Variables that measure the socio-economic characteristics of the present population group together less clearly because they form a more complicated and changeable set of measures; the distinctions are less clear cut.

As was mentioned in the Technical Introduction, the factor analysis was applied both to the ward data for the Conurbation and to the Birmingham enumeration district figures. Very similar factors were derived for the two areas – after all, half of the character of the Conurbation resides in the city. The different scales of investigation represented by the data, however, gave a different emphasis to the first five factors. This means that, in using the factor analysis to group variables into the five sections of the atlas, some factors highlight contrasts between different parts of the Conurbation at large, while others are more closely associated with the detailed social geography of the city of Birmingham. Table 5 illustrates this. The ordering of the factor numbers for the Conurbation and Birmingham is shown, together with their relationship with the sections of the atlas.

Table 5

Sections of atlas	Factor numbers	
I	Conurbation 1	Birmingham 3
II	Birmingham 1	Conurbation 5
III	Conurbation 3	Birmingham 5
IV	Conurbation 2	Birmingham 4
V	Birmingham 2	Conurbation 4

Thus, for example, Section I displays variables that are most strongly associated together at the level of the whole Conurbation but which have a relatively lower differentiating power in dealing with the more detailed figures for Birmingham (where they form factor 3). Section II, on the other hand, is particularly useful in differentiating areas within the city, using enumeration district data, but forms only the fifth factor, of relatively low differentiating power, with Conurbation ward data. In practice the fourth and fifth factors are much less satisfactory for our purposes than their predecessors. Our sections are principally based upon the first three factors for the conurbation (Sections I, III and IV) and the first two factors for Birmingham (Sections II and V). In both cases, of course, we examine the patterns for the individual variables over both areas. We are primarily interested in their distribution patterns; the factor analysis has simply been used as a guide to the organization of the atlas.

As has already been suggested, the two strongest factors for the Conurbation as a whole (in Sections I and IV) are based upon dwelling characteristics: the possession of basic amenities and types of tenure. These reflect the broad patterns of historical growth that distinguish areas most strongly at the Conurbation scale. The Birmingham-based factors (in Sections II and V) are more concerned with population and socio–economic characteristics. These form only the fourth and fifth factors in the Conurbation analysis and it appears that employment and occupations (Section II) and 'Zone of Transition' characteristics (Section V) are geographically too intricate and locally variable to be detected clearly by a ward analysis. In applying this double basis for the sections, therefore, we hope that something of the 'best of both worlds' has been attained in studying geographical patterns of variation at different scales. Finally, in Section III, patterns of age structure are investigated. This is based upon the weakest factor displayed, mainly because age characteristics are related to so many other housing and population variables. Nevertheless, for this very reason, the distribution of age groups is of particular importance in understanding changes in the urban system.

In each section, the variable that 'contributes' most towards the character of the factor has been presented. Other variables may be related positively to this 'primary' variable but many interesting measures will be *inversely* related to it. Thus each section contains inverse or negatively related variables.

Housing characteristics form the basis for the first section of this atlas, which we have entitled 'Affluence'. Unfortunately, of course, there is no information in the census that provides a direct measure of incomes or wealth. Housing quality provides an indirect index at the Conurbation scale, however; although, with increased incomes and a shortage of housing, many people today live in dwellings that may be poorer than their immediate earnings would allow. Section II groups together variables that are related to a key differentiator of people: employment. In the West Midlands the most significant question is whether workers are in manufacturing or non-manufacturing industries. As we have seen, this distinction is geographically more clearly related to other socio–economic variables in Birmingham than in the Conurbation at large. Section III plots the various age groups, together with associated variables concerned with employment. Section IV, 'Housing Tenure', again is concerned with classifying dwellings, this time according to the characteristics of buildings themselves (their ownership and size) rather than to the attributes that directly reflect the quality of life of their inhabitants. The final section of the atlas contains a mixed set of variables that group themselves around the primary variable of shared dwellings. This factor is obviously a mixture of housing and socio–economic variables and it mainly distinguishes a part of the population that is untypical in its living style – by circumstances or choice many people in these areas are not grouped into the 'average' family households and dwellings defined in Section I. As we shall see, this factor appears to identify the urban 'zone of transition' in Birmingham, details of which will be discussed more fully later.

Summary of sections

Section I	*'Affluence'*	Conurbation factor 1,	Birmingham factor 3
Section II	*Employment*	Conurbation factor 5,	Birmingham factor 1
Section III	*Age Structure*	Conurbation factor 3,	Birmingham factor 5
Section IV	*Housing Tenure*	Conurbation factor 2,	Birmingham factor 4
Section V	*'The Zone of Transition'*	Conurbation factor 4,	Birmingham factor 2

The range of each variable

In interpreting the maps it is important in each case to know the range of values being plotted. In most cases, this is a percentage figure (of the total population, of households or of dwellings) and the range may be the maximum possible, from 0 to 100 per cent. More often, however, the range of percentage values is much smaller. In certain cases (e.g. car ownership rates), the values are ratios other than percentages.

Shading categories

On each map there are eight shading categories. For every variable, the range has been equally subdivided into octiles. Thus in comparing maps, the same shading categories do not represent similar absolute percentage values. Whatever the subject of the map, however, the same shading symbol represents areas with the same value *in relation to the total range of values* for each variable. For example, the darkest shading on each map shows areas that fall into the top eighth of each variable's range. This convention aids comparison of the patterns for variables that have widely differing ranges of value. It was used in the *Atlas of London* (Reference 37), so that some comparison with that atlas should be possible.

Isopleth maps

As has been described in the Technical Introduction, the maps presented in the atlas are isopleth maps; the junction lines between different shading symbols join points of inferred

equal value. The method for inferring unknown values has been described in the Technical Introduction. The process of forming isopleths from areal data (as opposed to simply plotting the data on a ward or enumeration district map) involves a degee of generalization that is not serious where many known points of information are available and are evenly scattered. In some cases, however, wards or enumeration districts include areas with little population (e.g. in large parks, industrial areas and city centres) and the isopleth technique interpolates population into these areas, depending upon the pattern of surrounding areas. Examination of the land use maps (endpapers) in relation to the computer maps should permit allowance to be made for local distortions of this type.

A further consequence of using the isopleth technique is that it cannot very well represent sudden changes in the plotted characteristics. In providing a continuous 'surface' for each variable, the full range of values has to be represented even on parts of the maps where in fact there are extreme values in close proximity. In effect, this means that local trends in the surface should be interpreted with regard to the general pattern of surrounding areas and not be taken as a literal representation of the true value at any point.

The ten per cent sample

All of the data in this atlas is based upon the 1966 Sample Census. For many of the variables this sample is not sufficient at the enumeration district level to provide a reliable representation of the full population. This problem makes the use of individual enumeration district figures virtually impossible. Fortunately, in plotting the data on maps the general form of the patterns in itself provides a test of the consistency of the sample. Nevertheless, no significance should be placed upon localized nodes on the maps of Birmingham, attributable to only one enumeration district.

The histograms

A histogram (or frequency distribution curve) displays, for a range of values, the number of occurrences of different values within the range. The histograms that accompany each variable in this atlas show the numbers of wards of the whole Conurbation (marked C) and enumeration districts of Birmingham (marked B) on the vertical axis; the different values in the range are marked on the horizontal axis. In view of the differing ranges that are considered, both for the same variable between the Conurbation and Birmingham and for different variables, the scale of the horizontal axis is expressed in terms of the mean ($\overline{X}$) and standard deviation (SD) of each range, to allow comparisons. The standard deviation is a measure of the 'spread' of the whole set of values about the mean. One standard deviation may be defined as, 'the square root of the average of the squares of the deviations from the arithmetic mean'.

$$\sqrt{\frac{\Sigma(X - \overline{X})^2}{N}}$$

where: X represents a set of individual values

N is the total number of values under consideration.
This value has been calculated for each variable and is supplied with the histogram to allow the mean and standard deviation gradings to be interpreted.

The values of the means shown on the histograms may

Introduction

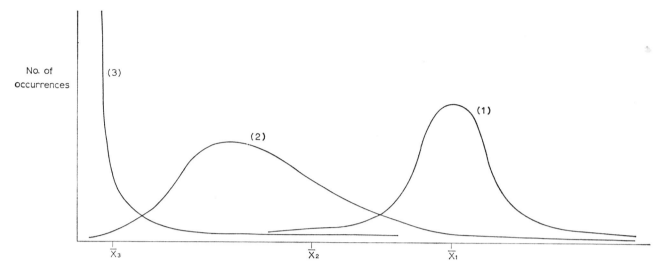

differ slightly from those mentioned in the text, taken from the published tables of the Census and intended to allow a general comparison with the representation of each variable for England and Wales. The means computed from the ward and enumeration-district data, given on each histogram, place equal weight upon all areas even though they differ in their numbers of population, households, and dwellings. Thus the published statistics presumably give a truer figure for the aggregate means of the Conurbation and Birmingham. The differences are generally of minor importance.

A 'normal' frequency distribution curve has values for the wards and enumeration districts grouped symmetrically about the mean (case 1 in the diagram). If the curve is asymmetrical, having a large proportion of values lower or higher than the mean, a 'skewed' distribution results (case 2 in the diagram). Such a histogram may be positively (as in case 2) or negatively skewed, according to whether the bulk of readings fall respectively to the left or right of the mean. In extreme cases of positive skewness of distribution (case 3) the most common value is very low (around zero). High values for these variables are thus rather unusual, possibly being concentrated into a few areas. The inverse would be true of an extreme negative skew (see, for example, variable 1). Thus, in general, different types of frequency curve for data applying to areas such as wards and enumeration districts provide a measure of the relative geographical dispersion of the different variables. Near normal frequency histograms are obtained for variables that measure geographically relatively common characteristics, in which variations from place to place are around some widely established 'average' (for the best examples, see variables 4, 6 and 12; also variables 9, 10, 11 and 16 are near normal). Highly skewed distributions, however, are found for variables that measure 'unusual' characteristics, often concentrated into only a few areas (see variables 2, 7, 15, 17, 18, 19, 21, 22). The majority of wards and enumeration districts score very low for these variables. The numbers of wards and enumeration districts is sufficiently large to ensure a normal sampling distribution. In spite of the skew of some of the data, therefore, significance tests can be reliably applied to the correlations.

Correlation

The correlation analysis that forms a guide in relating the occurrence of different variables is concerned with the charac-

teristics of *areal units*. In the Conurbation maps, these units are the 161 electoral wards, while in Birmingham they are the 451 enumeration district based areas. The correlation analysis tells us nothing directly about correlations between, for example, household characteristics or the attributes of particular groups of the population. High correlations indicate that areas with higher than average representations of variable A also tend to have higher than average representations of variable B. For example, the correlation of 0·6 between the percentage of shared dwellings in an area and the percentage of New Commonwealth immigrants, commented on in Section V, does *not* indicate that New Commonwealth immigrants share dwellings, nor even that they tend to live more in shared dwellings than the average (although this may be so). The correlation simply indicates that areas with more than 5 per cent of New Commonwealth immigrants also tend to have more than 10 per cent of shared dwellings. Obviously, the correlations may have a higher general 'causal' significance where the two variables have high percentage representations (i.e. where a nearly 0–100 per cent range is being considered).

Commentaries

To a large degree the maps are self-explanatory, once the range of each variable is established. The commentaries are designed to point out and discuss the salient points of the distributions and to suggest the significance of the principal correlations. A standardized format has been adopted in each commentary, although the discussion of certain variables is more protracted where this seems appropriate. The standardized format is as follows:

a) Definitions of the variable are explained.

b) 'Background' information, mostly taken from published census tables, indicates the occurrence of each index for England and Wales, for the Conurbation and for the city of Birmingham as a whole.

c) The range of the variable for the Conurbation wards and the Birmingham enumeration districts is indicated, together with the characteristics of the frequency distributions. In all cases histograms of the frequency distributions are also presented.

d) The geographical distribution on the two maps for each variable is described in relation to the geography of the Conurbation. (The road patterns that have been superimposed on each map allows comparison with the endpaper land use maps.

e) The principal correlations are pointed out. In the Conurbation ward analysis correlation coefficients of above 0·26 are statistically significant, while in the enumeration-district analysis of Birmingham significance is achieved by a coefficient of more than 0·16. Generally only correlation coefficients of more than 0·5 are discussed, although a table accompanies each variable which shows the more important correlations, including those below this level.

f) General comments about the significance of the patterns and relationships between variables provide a conclusion to each commentary.

Census definitions

The 1966 Sample Census enumerated the numbers present in each area of Great Britain on the night of the Census (24/25 April 1966), including people who normally live elsewhere. The sample aimed to include the population resident in every tenth structurally separate dwelling or small non-private establishment such as hotels, hospitals, etc. (Details of this sample and the estimated errors in representing the total number of households can be found in the introductions to the individual volumes of the Sample Census.)

Households: private

a) any group of persons, whether related or not, who live together and benefit from a common housekeeping, or

b) any person living alone who is responsible for providing his or her own meals (including breakfast)

Households must have at least one room, thus two persons sharing a room, regardless of whether they have a common housekeeping or share meals, are taken as one household.

Non-private establishments

Persons or groups of persons in non-private establishments such as hotels, boarding houses, hospitals, mental homes, old people's homes, children's homes, boarding schools, prisons, armed forces establishments, hostels, etc., were treated as separate households either:

a) if they were a family not normally depending upon the institution for the provision of meals, or

b) a person or group for whom the institution does not provide any daily meals

Dwellings

This refers to the buildings occupied by the enumerated population: a dwelling is a structurally separate accommodation with independent access to the street or to a public staircase or hall.

'Structurally separate' indicates that accommodation is contained behind its own front door (excluding, if necessary, bathrooms and w.c.s). 'Independent access to the street' is available if occupants can come and go without having access to anyone else's living quarters.

Dwellings include:

a) detached, semi-detached or terraced *houses*

b) *flats and maisonettes* in purpose-built blocks

c) *flats and maisonettes* in converted houses if each is contained behind its own front door. But *not* if one of the households occupies accommodation with more than one room opening onto a communal hall or landing; in this case the whole house was regarded as a single dwelling

d) *single rooms*, e.g. bed-sitting rooms, in converted houses only if they had their own bathroom and cooking facilities within the accommodation

e) the accommodation occupied by a private household within a *non-private establishment* even if it was not structurally separate and had access to the street only through the hotel, hospital, etc.

f) *houses attached to non-private establishments* only if occupied by private households, rather than guests, patients, inmates, etc.

Families

a) married couple with or without their never-married child(ren)

b) a mother or father with his or her never-married child(ren)

c) grandparents and their never-married grandchildren if there are no parents

'Families' include 'in-law', 'step-' and 'adopted' relationships but not foster relationships.

Other definitions will be provided where necessary as part of the commentaries for individual variables.

Atlas

Affluence

Source: 1966 Census Ward Data, Base Map prepared by The Centre for Urban and Regional Studies, University of Birmingham

Section I Conurbation factor 1 Affluence

Factor score, maximum included in highest level only

1	2	3	4	5	6	7	8
7·00–9·00	5·00–7·00	3·00–5·00	1·00–3·00	−1·00–1·00	−3·00– −1·00	−5·00– −3·00	−7·00– −5·00

The primary variable of this section notes the presence of households having the exclusive use of the basic physical household amenities (inside w.c., hot water and fixed bath). Most of the other variables that fall into this factor are negatively correlated with this; that is, they reflect the absence of basic amenities and its consequences. Thus, the areas of most deficient housing can be distinguished.

In tracing areas with a majority of adequately served family dwellings through these rather crude indices therefore, it is easier to say what characteristics they do *not* exhibit than to define their positive attributes. Essentially, they are not 'problem' areas; they do not have high proportions of young children, they have low unemployment and they have relatively few single persons living alone. The main variable that relates positively to the primary variable of this section, however, is interesting in itself, offering a measure of greater prosperity than average; car ownership per 100 households. Although little more detail about car ownership is available from the 1966 Sample Census at this scale of study, this index certainly justifies individual consideration and the 1971 Census plans to obtain a good deal more information about travelling habits. Another significant variable related to this factor for the Conurbation as a whole is one index of household tenure: the proportion of dwellings that are privately rented. Again, the relationship with the main variable is negative. In Birmingham, however, this variable falls into another factor and Section V provides a better context for the discussion of private renting (variable 20).

As we have pointed out in the Introduction, the factor that forms the basis for this section is the strongest that emerged from the statistical analysis of the Conurbation ward data. It formed factor 3 in the enumeration–district analysis of Birmingham. The distinctions that it draws between different areas are therefore most appropriate at the scale of the Conurbation. We have suggested that 'affluence', as a relative term implying broader aspects of living than simple income, provides the key to this factor. Thus, the Conurbation map of the factor scores shows basically its richer and poorer areas. The individual variables, both in this section and others, provide details of the many variations within the different zones but this map provides a composite summary of the Conurbation's most significant internal differences. The factor map provides a definition of the older areas of the Conurbation, mentioned in the Introduction, which are also generally the poorest areas (factor score above 1·0); of the wealthy areas of the newer conurbation (factor score under – 3·0); and, between these, of the intermediate areas.

Comparison with the land use map (endpapers, left) confirms the form of the poorest areas, constituting a central east to west belt from the zone of high density houses around Birmingham, through Smethwick, West Bromwich, Tipton, Wednesbury and Bilston to central Wolverhampton. The Willenhall–Walsall area on the north of the Black Country extends the zone in that direction, and in the south, where conditions are generally much better, Brierley Hill and Cradley Heath stand out as more isolated nodes of poor housing. On the other hand, as will become repeatedly emphasized throughout the atlas, the most affluent areas of the Conurbation are found on the north-east, in Sutton Coldfield, Streetly and southern Aldridge; on the south-east of the Conurbation, in Solihull; and to a lesser extent around the outer fringes of the Black Country, especially to the south-west of Stourbridge.

In this section, we have chosen to discuss four of the individual variables that contribute to this factor: the primary variable, defining areas with or without basic amenities; an index of the most physically deficient housing, the proportion of households without use of an inside w.c.; an index of the most affluent groups within the broad areas with adequate amenities, cars per 100 households; and an index which is grouped with this section in the analysis of Birmingham but which relates to Section II in the Conurbation as a whole, the percentage of married women working. This final variable provides both a perspective on the broader social consequences of the other variables in this section and also a link with the next section.

Conurbation factor 1			Other high factor loading		
Variable	Factor loading	Commun- ality	Section	Factor	Factor loading
2 Outside wc*	·818	·870	IV	3	−·333
32 Lacking hot water*	·815	·809			
1 All basic amenities*	−·801	·837	IV	2	−·309
24 Fertility ratio*	·658	·826	III	3	·588
20 Private renting*	·588	·713	V	4	·459
30 Travel to work	·585	·795	IV	2	−·533
3 Cars per household*	−·572	·535	II	5	·562
29 Households without families*	·565	·880	V	4	·587
			IV	2	−·334
			III	3	−·324
38 Unoccupied dwellings*	·562	·397			
22 New Commonwealth immigrants	·539	·740	V	4	·600
16 Dwelling size	·534	·861	IV	2	·602
39 Households occupied 1½ persons per room	·522	·827	V	4	·572
			IV	2	−·351
6 Unskilled group	·467	·888	IV	2	−·521
			II	5	−·574
41 Unemployment rate*	·466	·535	V	4	·417
			IV	2	−·378

Birmingham factor 3			Other high factor loading		
Variable	Factor loading	Commun- ality	Section	Factor	Factor loading
2 Outside wc*	−·814	·865	II	1	·406
1 All basic amenities*	·757	·846	IV	4	·350
32 Lacking hot water*	−·744	·762	II	1	·380
3 Cars per household*	·607	·662	II	1	−·505
40 Economically active	·564	·789	III	5	−·674
24 Fertility ratio*	−·520	·702	III	5	·496
4 Married women working	·495	·382			
41 Unemployment rate*	·466	·535	V	4	·418
			IV	2	−·378
29 Households without families*	−·463	·765	V	2	−·610
38 Unoccupied dwellings*	·437	·202	II	1	·500
30 Travel to work	−·391	·561	V	2	−·325
6 Unskilled group	−·356		II	1	·662
13 Owner-occupied	−·338	·888	IV	4	−·801

For complete list of variables, see Appendix I, p. 125.

* Principal variables in this factor

I Affluence Variable 1

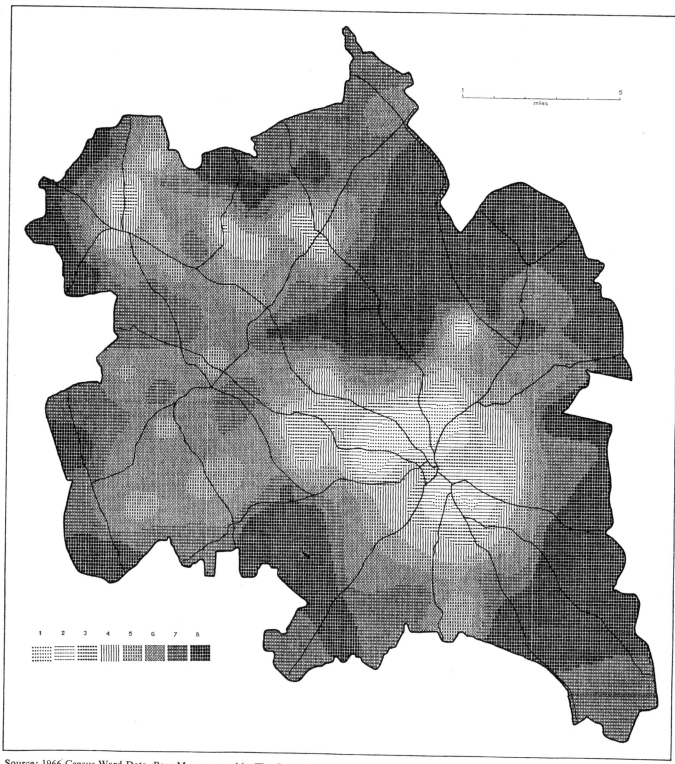

Source: 1966 Census Ward Data, Base Map prepared by The Centre for Urban and Regional Studies, University of Birmingham

1 Conurbation The percentage of households having exclusive use of all basic amenities

Maximum included in highest level only

1	2	3	4	5	6	7	8
19·00–29·00	29·00–39·00	39·00–49·00	49·00–59·00	59·00–69·00	69·00–79·00	79·00–89·00	89·00–99·00

Source: 1966 Enumeration-District Data, Base Map prepared by The Centre for Urban and Regional Studies, University of Birmingham

1 Birmingham The percentage of households having exclusive use of all basic amenities

Maximum included in highest level only

1	2	3	4	5	6	7	8
0·00–12·50	12·50–25·00	25·00–37·50	37·50–50·00	50·00–62·50	62·50–75·00	75·00–87·50	87·50–100·00

Variable 1

The percentage of households with exclusive use of all basic amenities (hot water, fixed bath and inside w c)

This index is a measure of the availability of adequate amenities (hot water, fixed bath and inside w.c.) in officially defined households. This particular measure of adequacy is not really enough, of course; modern definitions would include other measures than the possession of minimum basic amenities. The census is rather out of date in relying upon these physical indicators of household amenity, which originated decades ago in attempts to identify the worst of nineteenth-century slums. Space, lighting and heating standards, as well as modes of tenure and numbers of rooms might be invoked today. Some of these will be dealt with elsewhere in the atlas (see Sections IV and V).

As with all of the variables that we shall discuss, definitions are important, particularly the definitions of such special terms as 'households'. These have been summarized in the Introduction (p. 21) and in this case, for example, inadequate facilities may be suffered not only by 'families', in the accepted sense of the word, but also by other types of household, including single persons, both young and retired, living alone in rooms or flats, and related or unrelated persons sharing accommodation. As we shall emphasize in the last Section of this atlas, *shared* amenities are quite common amongst the various types of 'non-family' households but the *absence* of basic amenities is normally regarded as a clear sign of deficiency in housing.

In 1966, 72·4 per cent of the households in England and Wales had the exclusive use of the basic physical amenities of housing specified here. The large cities, of course, possess most of the poorest housing and Birmingham, for example, had only 63·6 per cent of its households in accommodation with all basic amenities. The Conurbation taken as a whole, however, possesses large areas of houses built during the last fifty years to a minimum standard and so nears the national average percentage, with 71·8 per cent.

The ranges of values within the Conurbation shown on the maps are considerable and, although Birmingham contains the worst areas lacking standard amenities, the Black Country also fares badly in its central areas. The data for the Conurbation as a whole shows some wards with as little as 19 per cent of houses with all basic amenities and others with as much as 99 per cent. In Birmingham the enumeration districts show the full range, from 0 to 100 per cent. The frequency distribution show a marked negative skew in both cases (see histogram).

In the Conurbation, the areas with high proportions of houses with all basic amenities. (greater than 79 per cent of households) are predictably on its periphery. Listing them in clockwise order from the north, they include the northern part of West Bromwich, Great Barr, Streetly and Sutton Coldfield on the north; the east and south-eastern suburbs of Birmingham; Solihull, to the south-east of the city; the south-west of Birmingham and Halesowen in the south of the Black Country; southern Stourbridge; western Brierley Hill, around Kingswinford; the western parts of Wolverhampton, including Tettenhall; and, on the north of the Black Country, the north Wednesfield–Bloxwich belt. These areas, many of them fully built up only during the past twenty years, are augmented by areas where adequate household amenities are predominant in Sedgley, the southern part of Wolverhampton and west and east of central Dudley. The low areas are mainly in the central and inner wards of Birmingham, extending to parts of Smethwick and West Bromwich and near the centres of other Black Country towns, in Walsall, Wolverhampton and Willenhall. This map very clearly establishes the basic dichotomy between 'inner' and 'outer' areas of the Conurbation, described in outline in the Introduction

In Birmingham, as with all the variables, the details provided

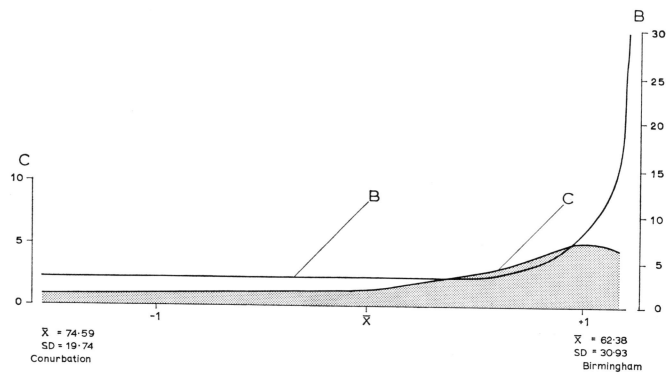

X̄ = 74·59
SD = 19·74
Conurbation

X̄ = 62·38
SD = 30·93
Birmingham

by the enumeration-district data presents a more intricate and fragmented picture of the distribution of basic amenities. Nevertheless, the general impression gained from the ward map of the Conurbation is confirmed, with the central areas badly deficient in basic amenities and even some of the suburban areas with only moderate proportions of properly served households. Thus the ring of poor living conditions (with less than 25 per cent of households having exclusive use of the basic amenities) concentrates around the city centre in the zone that is now the subject of extensive redevelopment schemes. Outside these areas, wide areas of the city also have less than the median proportion of adequately served households (50 per cent).

The areas of good housing conditions include the eastern lobe of the city, from Sheldon to Castle Bromwich; parts of Hall Green on the south-east; the south-western parts of the city, except for certain areas around the older settlements such as Harborne, Selly Oak and Cotteridge (near Bournville); and, on the north, Handsworth Wood–Kingstanding. Breaks in this outer ring include parts of Erdington and eastern Kingstanding on the north; Yardley Wood, Billesley and parts of Acocks Green on the south-east; and, of course, the areas of Handsworth, Winson Green and Ladywood, adjacent to Smethwick on the western side of the city centre. In the central parts of the city, where the poorest housing has been traditional, nodes of good housing show where the redevelopment areas are beginning to make their mark. In 1966, however, even after fifteen years of effort, large areas on the map still show a vast predominance of poor housing without the basic amenities. Many areas had been virtually cleared by demolition in 1966, however, with very small populations remaining, and other areas are mainly industrial in character with only small pockets of old housing. Thus the map gives a misleading impression of the geographical extent of the housing problem that remains in Birmingham, while emphasizing its local intensity. The problems of Winson Green, Aston, Bordesley and Balsall Heath will not be completely

solved until the next phase of redevelopment in the city is completed (Reference 28).

Areas where the possession of basic amenities is normal are overwhelmingly found where small family houses have been built since the First War. The main distinction to be drawn within this class of generally adequate houses is probably between those built before and after the Second World War. A wide range of social classes is also accommodated in them, of course, and they range in character from the inter-war council estates of Kingstanding to the most expensive houses in the region, found, for example, in Solihull or Edgbaston. Poor housing conditions in the Conurbation are related most directly to the age of the buildings. Old houses were either inadequate when they were originally built or were intended for larger families than are normal today, so that they have been subdivided into multiple dwellings without adequate individual amenities (see Section V).

The correlation analysis of all other variables indicates that the highest correlations with this variable are inverse; with the use of outside w.c.s only (cf. map of variable 2) and with the absence of hot water. These two characteristics clearly identify the problems of housing in the low areas on the maps of this variable. In the Conurbation, other characteristics of poor housing areas include high proportions of privately rented property (variable 20), of New Commonwealth and Irish immigrants (variables 22 and 21), of high proportions of young children (variables 9 and 24) and of single-person households (variable 29). In Birmingham the greater complexity of the detailed enumeration-district pattern provides rather lower correlations but the same group of variables are involved. In the city, as we have already noted, the group of variables discussed in Section V are more important and the distinctions between the traditional working-class areas of bad housing, now undergoing redevelopment, and the more recently developed 'zone of transition' are more clearly seen. These variations can be more fully investigated through the examination of the data summarized in this section and in Section V.

Conurbation

Variable	Stepwise multiple correlation	Simple correlation
2 Outside wc	·69	−·69
14 Council renting	·97	·41
32 Lacking hot water		−·68
20 Private renting		−·66
22 New Commonwealth immigrants		−·60
21 Irish immigrants		−·53
24 Fertility ratio		−·53
29 Households without families		−·53

Birmingham

Variable	Stepwise multiple correlation	Simple correlation
2 Outside wc	·76	−·76
14 Council renting	·95	·23
33 Sharing wc	·97	−·25
32 Lacking hot water		−·71
24 Fertility ratio		−·62
15 Multiple dwelling purpose-built		·57
39 Households occupied 1½+ persons per room		−·47
22 New Commonwealth immigrants		−·45
21 Irish immigrants		−·42

I Affluence Variable 2

Source: 1966 Census Ward Data, Base Map prepared by The Centre for Urban and Regional Studies, University of Birmingham

2 Conurbation The percentage of households which have the use of an outside wc only

Maximum included in highest level only

1	2	3	4	5	6	7	8
0·0–9·00	9·00–18·00	18·00–27·00	27·00–36·00	36·00–45·00	45·00–54·00	54·00–63·00	63·00–72·00

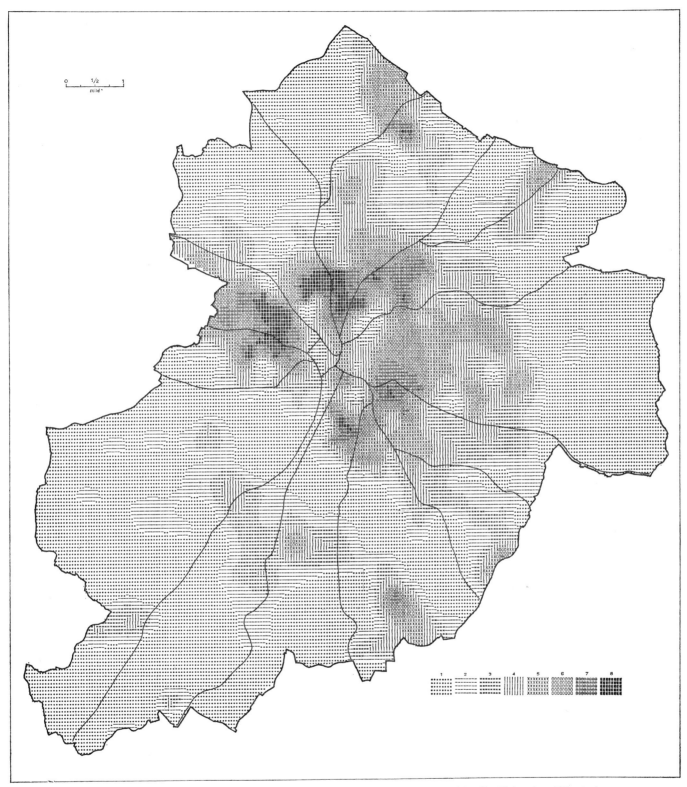

Source: 1966 Enumeration-District Data, Base Map prepared by The Centre for Urban and Regional Studies, University of Birmingham

2 Birmingham The percentage of households which have the use of an outside w c only

Maximum included in highest level only

1	2	3	4	5	6	7	8
0.00–12.50	12.50–25.00	25.00–37.50	37.50–50.00	50.00–62.50	62.50–75.00	75.00–87.50	87.50–100.00

Variable 2

The percentage of households with the use of an outside w c only

The patterns formed by the areas where many households lack the various basic amenities discussed under variable 1 are very similar in the Conurbation and Birmingham for each individual amenity. Here we show the maps of households lacking an inside w.c. to represent these patterns. Households lacking hot water or a fixed bath are found in the same areas and it is clear that the various census indices of housing deficiency measure different aspects of the same feature. Rather different patterns of occurence emerge when considering shared housing amenities and these will be examined in some detail in Section V. The absence of hot water, a fixed bath and an inside w.c., particularly in combination in the same types of housing, has generally been regarded as among the most shocking aspects of nineteenth century slum housing. It is likely that, as the worst of the slums are cleared and the basic amenities become universal, other indices, more sensitive to the positive qualities of housing, and the needs of families living in them, will have to be devised.

A comparison of this section and Section V will confirm that the absence of basic amenities is not the sole criterion of bad housing; generally speaking, the manner and intensity of their use is also important. The 'sharing' indices, exemplified in this atlas by variable 18, fall into another factor grouped with the private renting of dwellings and recent immigration. They do not appear in this factor which draws the distinction between 'adequate' and 'inadequate' amenities in the sense that has been accepted since the late nineteenth century. It seems that the distinction has emerged between the 'old' working-class slums of the Conurbation and the 'new' problem areas, where large, formerly middle-class houses have been sub-divided and overcrowded by various types of newcomer.

There are, however, no hard and fast distinctions to be made. Although much slum clearance and rebuilding has taken place in the Conurbation, especially in Birmingham, 22 per cent of Conurbation households in 1966 (165,000 persons) still only had use of an outside w.c. In Birmingham this proportion was 27·8 per cent (92,000 persons) compared with the average for England and Wales of 18·0 per cent. The maps and histogram show how concentrated the problem is into

certain areas, however. Thus, although many wards in the Conurbation have virtually no households in this category, some around central Birmingham still have above 63 per cent and in the more detailed analysis of enumeration districts for the city, some have 100 per cent of their houses in this category. In the Conurbation, the 'old' areas developed in the mid-nineteenth century and described in outline in the Introduction stand out quite clearly. The incidence of this inadequacy is most intense around central Birmingham, and other towns in the Black Country, such as Smethwick, Walsall, Willenhall and Wolverhampton also emerge as areas of poor housing conditions and relative poverty. In Birmingham, the girdle of slum housing, repeated on other maps of deficient basic amenities, marks the zone of present redevelopment. Many of the areas have undergone extensive demolition, and rebuilding to modern standards is already biting into the continuity of the slum belt. Nevertheless, large areas of Aston, to the north of the city centre, Nechells to the north-east, Bordesley Green to the east, Balsall Heath to the south and Ladywood and Winson Green on the west, had more than 62·5 per cent of their households without inside w.c.s in 1966. In addition certain suburban areas, in the north, east and south of the city, had nodes of houses without inside w.c.s but these do not appear on the maps of other amenities that are absent, such as hot water, and probably result from localized styles of relatively recent housing where w.c.s were built outside.

The correlation analysis confirms that areas where households generally depend upon outside w.c.s also lack hot water provision (variable 32). In addition, unskilled workers (variable 6) are in consistently greater proportions than elsewhere and rely upon public transport to travel to work (variable 30). Overcrowding (variable 39, households with more than 1½ persons per room) is higher than average, as is the representation of single-person households (variable 29) and immigrant groups from the New Commonwealth (variable 22). The strong inverse correlations, as might be expected, are with car ownership (variable 3), owner-occupied housing (variable 13) and professional and managerial workers (variable 7).

We have no direct measure of affluence or wealth from the census. It simply provides us with a range of data about the

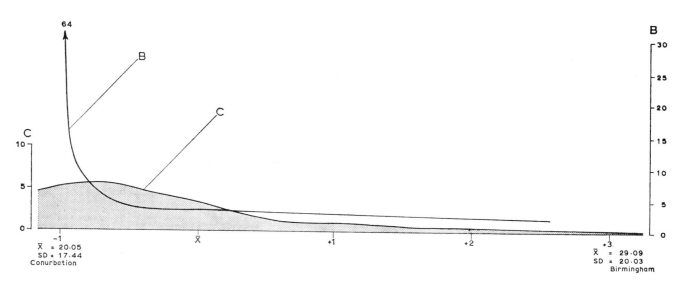

X̄ = 20·05
SD = 17·44
Conurbation

X̄ = 29·09
SD = 20·03
Birmingham

styles of living of people from different areas and in different economic pursuits. If a more direct measure of family poverty were available, however, it is very likely that the areas with high representation on these maps would be the poorest.

Similarly, within the wide areas of the Conurbation having adequate housing, a useful index of the particularly well-off groups would be car ownership, and it is to this measure that we shall turn our attention in variable 3.

Conurbation	Stepwise multiple correlation	Simple correlation
Variable		
30 Travel to work	·76	·76
1 All basic amenities	·86	—·69
14 Council renting	·97	·33
20 Private renting	·98	·46
33 Sharing wc	·99	·21
32 Lacking hot water		·81
3 Cars per household		—·73
6 Unskilled group		·70
29 Households without families		·64
39 Households occupied 1½+ persons per room		·64
13 Owner-occupied		—·58
7 Professional and managerial group		—·53
41 Unemployment rate		·50
22 New Commonwealth immigrants		·49

Birmingham	Stepwise multiple correlation	Simple correlation
Variable		
1 All basic amenities	·75	—·75
14 Council renting	·96	·40
33 Sharing wc	·98	(not significant)
13 Owner-occupied	·99	—·54
32 Lacking hot water		·83
3 Cars per household		—·57
6 Unskilled group		·51
24 Fertility ratio		·51
30 Travel to work		·48
7 Professional and managerial group		—·48
9 Age 0–14		·46
5 Manufacturing workers		·41

Variable 32, Lacking hot water, was eliminated from the multiple correlation matrix because of multicollinearity

Source: 1966 Census Ward Data, Base Map prepared by The Centre for Urban and Regional Studies, University of Birmingham

3 Conurbation The number of cars per 100 households

Maximum included in the highest level only

1	2	3	4	5	6	7	8
18·00–30·50	30·50–43·00	43·00–55·50	55·50–68·00	68·00–80·50	80·50–93·00	93·00–105·50	105·50–118·0

Source: 1966 Enumeration-District Data, Base Map prepared by The Centre for Urban and Regional Studies, University of Birmingham

3 Birmingham The number of cars per 100 households

Maximum included in highest level only

1	2	3	4	5	6	7	8
6·00–18·00	18·00–30·00	30·00–42·00	42·00–54·00	54·00–66·00	66·00–78·00	78·00–90·00	90·00–102·00

35

Variable 3

The number of cars per 100 households

This index provides a gross measure of the rate of car ownership. Access to the use of a motor vehicle is becoming regarded as a necessity for modern living, particularly in the more prosperous section of the population. As such, measures of car ownership indicate the inverse of the poor housing conditions discussed under variable 2. Indeed, they are often used as a satisfactory substitute for direct measures of personal and household wealth. Comparison with the two maps of variable 1 shows how car ownership picks out areas within the zones of broadly adequate housing, revealing the most prosperous parts of the Conurbation. There are close similarities between the maps of car ownership and those of professional and managerial workers, variable 7 in the next section of the atlas.

Car ownership is not yet a majority attribute for households in England and Wales; in 1966, 45·8 per cent of them had use of at least one car. In the West Midlands Conurbation the proportion was 44·1 per cent and in Birmingham the rate was only 41·1 per cent. Allowing for the possession by some households of more than one car, car ownership rates in 1966 were 52·8 per 100 households nationally, 52·0 for the Conurbation and only 45·0 in Birmingham. The maps for the Conurbation and Birmingham show how locally variable this index is, however, ranging from 18 to 118 in the wards of the Conurbation and from 6 to 102 in the enumeration districts of the city. The highest level is lower in Birmingham than in the Conurbation at large, unlike most indices discussed in this atlas where the detailed enumeration-district figures for the city are more extreme than the generalized figures for wards. Nowhere in Birmingham, however, does car ownership reach the level of places such as Solihull or Sutton Coldfield, even allowing for the different geographical size of the data units.

The high areas of car ownership (greater than 93 per 100 households) are in northern Sutton Coldfield and Streetly, in Solihull and the southern part of Stourbridge. Areas of high, though lesser concentration fringe the eastern and western edges of the Conurbation. In Birmingham, where levels of car ownership are generally lower than in these high areas of the Conurbation, the main concentrations are found in the north-west to south-east Edgbaston–Moseley–Yardley Wood zone. This zone emerges on other maps of relatively high living standard indices (e.g. variable 7, professional and managerial workers). High car ownership is also found in Kings Norton,

on the south of the city and Handsworth Wood on the north-west. Higher than the median representation (54 cars per 100 households) is found in much broader areas of the city's suburbs, however, especially in the south-west, north-west and east. This pattern corresponds quite closely to that of houses with all basic amenities, variable 1, both for the Conurbation and Birmingham. The correlation analysis produces a long list of other variables that are related to car ownership in their distributions throughout the Conurbation. High car ownership is *inversely* related to the proportions of unskilled workers in an area (variable 6), the use of public transport to travel to work (variable 30), poor housing conditions, as defined in discussing the last variable (variable 2), the proportions of females of working age who work (variable 34), single and two-person households (variables 29 and 36), the proportion of Commonwealth immigrants (variable 22), the proportion of workers in manufacturing (variable 5) and the level of unemployment (variable 41). Positive correlations include those with areas of professional and managerial workers (variable 7), workers in the distributive industries (variable 27), high proportions of persons who have moved into the local authority in the 5 years before 1966 (the most important moves in this category have been to the wealthy satellite boroughs on the periphery of the Conurbation (see variable 17) and the owner-occupation of houses (variable 13)). In Birmingham most of the significant correlations are negative – low car ownership being found in areas of poor housing, high proportions of young children, unskilled workers, manufacturing employment and high proportions of immigrants.

At the scale of the Conurbation, the ownership of cars today can be related to family wealth, access to alternative modes of transport (especially public transport) and space standards of living and environment which may allow the parking, garaging and ready use of motor vehicles. These conditions favour the outer parts of the Conurbation on all counts. In a city like Birmingham, however, the small-scale patterns are obviously affected by its historically developed form (see variable 7, discussion) and to the socio–economic classes that live in different areas. The West Midlands Transport Study (Reference 9) explored transportation variables in some detail. One important factor arising from their survey was that 7 per cent of the cars based in their study area (which included all of the Conurbation and parts of the surrounding counties) were rented or supplied by employers and that these were heavily concentrated into Solihull and Sutton Coldfield,

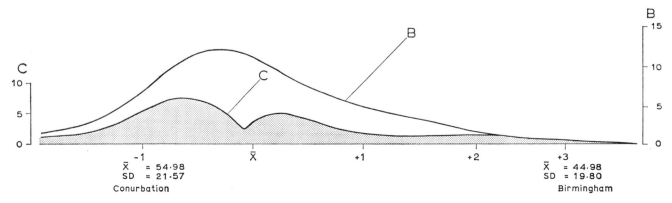

$\bar{X}$ = 54·98
SD = 21·57
Conurbation

$\bar{X}$ = 44·98
SD = 19·80
Birmingham

36

the two areas of major concentration on our maps. Again, the importance of socio–economic characteristics are evident: certain groups tend to work in jobs which provide cars which can be used by the family. Another important feature emphasized by the Transport Study (p. 36), was that the densities of cars per unit area in the outer parts of the Conurbation were much lower than in many inner parts of the Conurbation. Thus high population densities, even with low rates of car ownership contribute heavily to the congestion problems of the central parts of the Conurbation. The West Midlands Transport Study also suggested that car-owning households had above-average numbers of employed persons, including more wives and older children. This relationship between car ownership and the earning habits of families is obviously a circular one, but this analysis suggests that the employment of women in areas of high car ownership is in fact significantly lower than elsewhere.

Looking ahead, the Transport Study (p. 164) foresaw 820,000 cars being owned in its study area by 1981 compared with 388,000 in 1964. 69 per cent of households would have access to the use of a car, with 28 per cent having two cars or more (compared with only 5 per cent in 1964). Most of the outer parts of the Conurbation would have 75 per cent or more of their households owning cars and only parts of inner Birmingham and Smethwick would have as few as 45 per cent. The significance of such indices for the future planning of the region cannot be overestimated.

Conurbation

Variable	Stepwise multiple correlation	Simple correlation
6 Unskilled group	·84	—·84
1 All basic amenities	·87	·44
7 Professional and managerial group	·92	·82
11 Age 65+	·94	—·32
30 Travel to work	·95	—·76
2 Outside w c		—·73
32 Lacking hot water		—·67
34 Female employment		—·64
29 Households without families		—·63
27 Distribution workers		·61
5 Manufacturing workers		—·59
13 Owner-occupied		·59
39 Households occupied 1½+ persons per room		—·58
22 New Commonwealth immigrants		—·56
17 Migration into local authority		·56
36 2-person households		—·53
35 Sharing sink and stove		—·50
41 Unemployment rate		—·50

Birmingham

Variable	Stepwise multiple correlation	Simple correlation
1 All basic amenities	·64	·64
7 Professional and managerial group	·79	—·60
30 Travel to work	·80	—·60
32 Lacking hot water		—·62
2 Outside w c		—·58
6 Unskilled group		—·57
24 Fertility ratio		—·55
5 Manufacturing workers		—·49
27 Distribution workers		·49
39 Households occupied 1½+ persons per room		—·46
22 New Commonwealth immigrants		—·45
21 Irish immigrants		—·45

I Affluence Variable 4

Source: 1966 Census Ward Data, Base Map prepared by The Centre for Urban and Regional Studies, University of Birmingham

4 Conurbation The percentage of married women working

Maximum included in highest level only

1	2	3	4	5	6	7	8
32·00–34·75	34·75–37·50	37·50–40·25	40·25–43·00	43·00–45·75	45·75–48·50	48·50–51·25	51·25–54·00

Source: 1966 Enumeration-District Data, Base Map prepared by The Centre for Urban and Regional Studies, University of Birmingham

4 Birmingham The percentage of married women working

Maximum in highest level only

1	2	3	4	5	6	7	8
20·00–27·00	27·00–34·00	34·00–41·00	41·00–48·00	48·00–55·00	55·00–62·00	62·00–69·00	69·00–76·00

Variable 4

The percentage of married women working

This index is very significant for socio–economic analysis, since it reflects, on one hand, a major variable in the labour force of an area, and on the other hand, the importance of additions to family income that arise from wives working. There are also other, more subtle implications for the character and cohesiveness of the family unit. Female activity rates (the proportion of women of working age who work) are high in the West Midlands and particularly so in the Conurbation. In local areas they are the result of a variety of influences at work upon the reserves of women potential workers. The social and age structure of the population provides part of any general explanation, while geographical location in relation to employment opportunities may also be significant. A large and fairly constant proportion of unmarried women work, so that the main variations in female activity rates are due to variations in married women working. In fact, the maps of these two variables show very similar patterns. Some married women have to work whenever possible for economic reasons. Many others do not need to work and there remains wide scope for choice. Age plays a part – older women with grown-up children have relatively high activity rates; economic aspiration may influence the choice – activity rates among married women are high in lower-middle-class groups; and, as we have mentioned, opportunity within a reasonable distance and with good transport facilities may also be significant.

In 1966, the average percentage of married women working in England and Wales was 38·4 per cent. In the West Midlands Conurbation the figure was 44·8 per cent and in Birmingham it was as high as 46·2 per cent. Clearly, as well as the operation of a complex of local variables, there is a marked regional propensity for women to work in the West Midlands. As far as can be judged from the limited data available (see Reference 19, chapter 6) virtually every social class and age cohort in the West Midlands Conurbation has a higher than average proportion of married women working. Unlike certain other parts of Britain with high proportions of female employment, such as the textile areas, there is no predominance in the West Midlands of specifically female-employing jobs; the general shortage of labour has meant that women have occupied jobs formerly worked by men, particularly in service occupations, the metal goods and engineering industries, clerical work and retail sales.

In the Conurbation as a whole, the range of ward values is from 32 per cent to 54 per cent and in Birmingham the enumeration-district values spread from 20 per cent to 76 per cent of the resident married women who are working. The highest values are mostly found in the industrial Black Country part of the Conurbation. A central area covers Smethwick, Oldbury, Tipton and West Bromwich, including areas of relatively modern housing in the Great Barr area. To the north-west, the Wolverhampton–Willenhall area is important and in the south of the Black Country, the Cradley Heath–Halesowen area also has more than 45 per cent of its married women working. In Birmingham the detailed pattern is quite compli-cated, but the Conurbation map shows how the central areas, the south-western and north-eastern suburbs are predominant.

On the enumeration-district map of Birmingham, the areas with most married females working are in the vicinity of the city centre where there are many opportunities for employment in offices and shops for women living nearby. The numbers living in this area, however, must be very small. The major sector of married female employment in the city is for service workers such as cleaners and waitresses and many of the 32,000 jobs enumerated in this class of occupations in the 1966 census must be located around the centre of the city. 22,000 of these were part-time jobs. Clerical jobs for married women amounted to 24,000 (10,000 part-time) and sales jobs to 13,500 (7,000 part-time.) No very strong pattern of concentration emerges in this distribution for the rest of the city (the frequency distribution is near normal); a number of relatively small nodes occur in the suburbs without displaying a consistent pattern: it appears that at this scale of analysis, local circum-

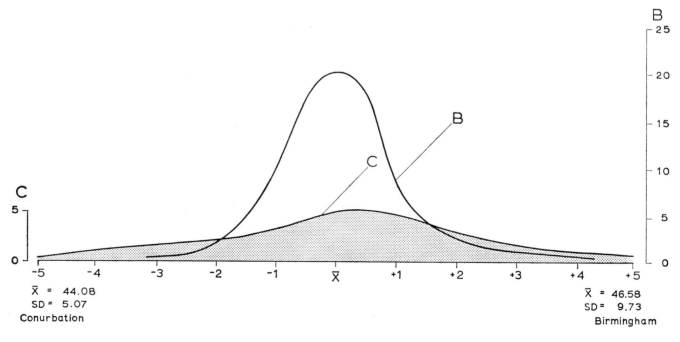

X̄ = 44.08
SD = 5.07
Conurbation

X̄ = 46.58
SD = 9.73
Birmingham

stances of social, demographic and economic structure are more important than broad location as a general factor. The main nodes are: to the west of the city centre, along and to the south of Hagley Road in Edgbaston. This is mainly occupied by professional workers, many of them middle-aged couples. North of this area, in Ladywood, there appears to be a very different, mainly working-class area, at present subject to slum clearance schemes, with industrial premises closely mixed into the residential fabric. Further south-west, Harborne provides a certain amount of local employment and also has a predominance of families of a suitable age and social class to encourage high proportions of the married women to work. On the south-west borders of the city, new housing areas, mainly built by the city council, in Bartley Green, Northfield and Kings Norton, have high levels of working among married women in spite of their generally young age structure and large numbers of children (variable 9). On the east of the city, Sheldon also has high values.

In the correlation and factor analysis this variable occupies an unusual situation. For the city of Birmingham it falls into the factor that has formed the basis of this section: related to housing conditions and general levels of affluence. As we have suggested, however, this association is rather a weak one. In the Conurbation ward analysis the proportion of married

women working seems to be related more with the Section II variables: to the occurrence of different occupation classes and workers in different industries. It is entirely characteristic of this complicated measure that it should exhibit different patterns of association at different scales of analysis. In the Conurbation as a whole, the most interesting significant correlations are with the proportions of residents in an area working in manufacturing (variable 5) and with the proportions of males who are skilled workers (variable 37). The association with manufacturing employment confirms the results of a more generally based analysis of the Conurbation's female activity rates by Lomas and Wood (Reference 19). Evidently, families in the skilled manual socio-economic groups have the highest married female activity rates. This is partly a function of their typical age structure and partly a matter of increasing the family income in order to satisfy certain economic aspirations such as car ownership, already discussed under variable 3.

In Birmingham no really significant variables have similar patterns of occurrence to married women working and this seems to confirm that at the very localized detail of enumeration-districts' study this variable is the product of a complex of conditions that produce very haphazard geographical patterns.

Conurbation		
Variable	Stepwise multiple correlation	Simple correlation
5 Manufacturing workers	·47	·47
11 Age 65+	·62	−·46
34 Female employment	·86	·44
40 Economically active		·53
37 Skilled workers		·47
16 Dwelling size		−·46
7 Professional and managerial group		−·43
42 Persons per room		·42

Birmingham		
Variable	Stepwise multiple correlation	Simple correlation
34 Female employment	·45	·45
11 Age 65+	·72	−·44
40 Economically active		·50
15 Multiple dwellings purpose-built		·36
1 All basic amenities		·32

Variable 40, Economically active ratio, has been eliminated from the multiple correlation matrix because of multicollinearity.

II Introduction

This factor groups together variables that primarily provide some measure of occupations. It includes measures of the proportions of resident population working in manufacturing, in distribution and in government service (these three indices are, of course, interdependent); the proportions that are professional and managerial, and those that are skilled and unskilled workers (again, these four are defined according to the same classification system). The more interesting, apparently more 'independent' associations with this factor include the proportion of females/males (lower in areas of manufacturing workers); the proportion of households with two or more families (this is most marked in the Black Country), and, in Birmingham specifically, the proportion of married women that work (discussed already in variable 4).

Unfortunately, we have no measure of the actual locations of jobs at either the ward or enumeration-district scale of analysis; the employment characteristics of the population are measured only in relation to the places of residence of individuals.

From the factor analysis it is clear that employment and occupation measures provide a much more effective distinction between areas within the city of Birmingham than within the Conurbation as a whole. In the statistical analysis of the Birmingham enumeration-district data this factor was the strongest in the city and the weakest of those examined (the fifth factor) in the Conurbation at large, It has already been suggested in the Introduction that probably it is the finer detail of the Birmingham analysis that allows the distinctions traced by this factor to be identified. A glance at the map of the factor scores in Birmingham confirms how locally variable is the pattern that has been detected – ward boundaries are too crude to pick up these variations.

Obviously the factor provides a broad distinction between the inner and outer areas of the city and between the city centre and Edgbaston and the rest of the inner areas. The composite measure that the factor provides takes account in Birmingham of employment in manufacturing, unskilled socio-economic groupings, low ratios of females/males and high proportions of married women working. These characteristics come together most closely (factor score more than 2) in the inner belt of slums around the city centre (Sections I and IV) and also in certain of the surrounding areas of the 'zone of transition', discussed in Section V. Most of Aston, to the north of the city centre, is included; on the east, a north to south belt from Saltley to Small Heath; on the south, Spark-brook and Balsall Heath are prominent; and on the west most of Ladywood, Winson Green and the inner parts of Hands-worth stand out. These are all socially deprived areas of one type or another and, for the city, this factor is clearly tracing the same type of 'poor' area that was identified for the Conurbation as a whole in the factor map that introduced Section I. Evidently, as might be expected, the detailed analysis of the city allows distinctions of affluence to be related directly to economic classifications of occupations and socio-economic groupings.

In this section we therefore have a grouping of economically significant variables. The patterns for the Conurbation as a whole, as we shall see in discussing individual variables, provides less clear-cut distinctions between areas, but this is probably due more to the scale of analysis than any real distinction in the importance of the indices. Again we have presented four variables to represent the factor; employment in manufacturing and allied groups; the proportions of unskilled workers, and the proportions of professional and managerial workers, to represent the extremes of the socio-economic variations that forms part of this factor; and the percentage of households with two or more families – a variable that is less obviously related to the others within the factor and which also is particularly distinctive of the Black Country, rather than of Birmingham.

Conurbation factor 5 Variable	Factor loading	Commun-ality	Other high factor loading		
			Section	Factor	Factor loading
5 Manufacturing workers*	−·880	·876			
27 Distribution workers*	·864	·873			
7 Professional and managerial group*	·736	·879	IV	2	·518
4 Married women working	−·628	·658	I	1	−·447
6 Unskilled group*	−·574	·888	IV	2	−·521
			I	1	·467
3 Cars per household	·562	·535	I	1	−·572
28 Government workers*	·546	·339			
23 Sex ratio*	·532	·423	III	3	−·305
37 Skilled workers*	·523	·488	V	4	−·301
40 Economically active	−·518	·870	III	3	−·703
			I	1	−·303
8 Households with 2+ families*	−·485	·470	IV	2	−·443
42 Persons per room	−·472	·935	IV	2	−·704
			III	3	·457
19 Multiple dwellings converted	·432	·687	V	4	·677

Birmingham factor 1 Variable	Factor loading	Commun-ality	Other high factor loading		
			Section	Factor	Factor loading
27 Distribution workers*	−·863	·765			
5 Manufacturing workers*	·857	·766			
7 Professional and managerial group*	−·804	·753			
6 Unskilled group*	·662	·710	I	3	−·356
23 Sex ratio*	−·553	·411			
42 Persons per room	·551	·819	IV	4	·565
			III	5	·370
3 Cars per household	−·505	·662	I	3	·607
30 Travel to work	·500	·561	I	3	−·391
			V	2	−·325
28 Governmental workers*	−·384	·182			
8 Households with 2+ families*	·343	·216	III	5	−·303

* Principal variables in this factor.

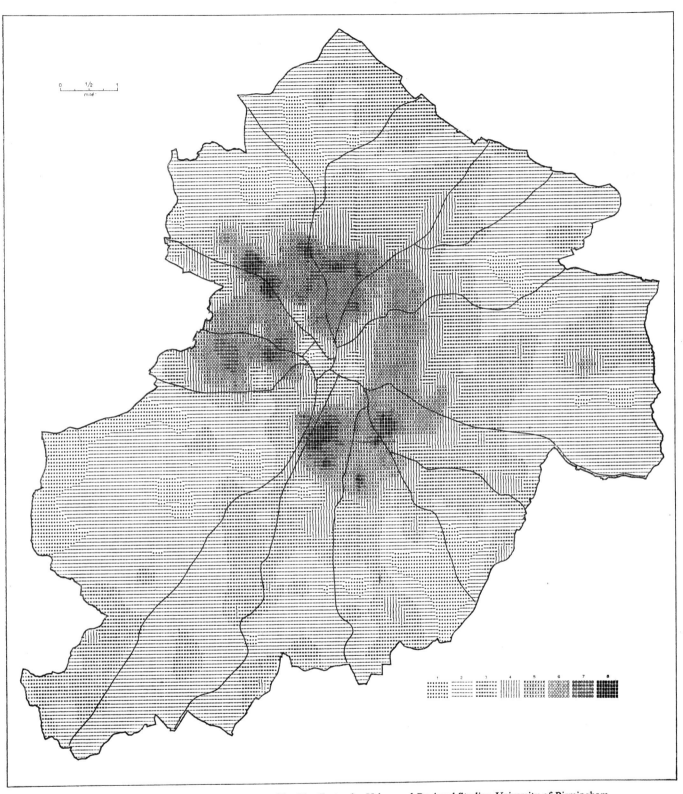

Source: 1966 Enumeration-District Data, Base Map prepared by The Centre for Urban and Regional Studies, University of Birmingham

Section II Birmingham factor 1 Employment

Factor score, maximum included in highest level only

1	2	3	4	5	6	7	8
−5·00− −3·25	−3·25− −1·50	−1·50−0·25	0·25−2·00	2·00−3·75	3·75−5·50	5·50−7·25	7·25−9·00

Source: 1966 Census Ward Data, Base Map prepared by The Centre for Urban and Regional Studies, University of Birmingham

5 Conurbation The percentage of the economically active population working in manufacturing, construction and public utility industries

Maximum included in highest level only

1	2	3	4	5	6	7	8
41·00–46·00	46·00–51·00	51·00–56·00	56·00–61·00	61·00–66·00	66·00–71·00	71·00–76·00	76·00–81·00

Source: 1966 Enumeration-District Data, Base Map prepared by The Centre for Urban and Regional Studies, University of Birmingham

5 Birmingham The percentage of the economically active population working in manufacturing, construction and public utility industries

Maximum included in highest level only

1	2	3	4	5	6	7	8
27·00–**34·00**	34·00–41·00	41·00–48·00	48·00–55·00	55·00–62·00	62·00–69·00	69·00–76·00	76·00–83·00

Variable 5

The percentage of the economically active population working in manufacturing, construction and public utility industries

One of the most distinctive features of the West Midlands Conurbation is the high proportion of its employed population working in manufacturing industry. In fact, with its relatively low proportions of service and mining employment, the West Midlands relies for work more heavily than any other British region upon manufacturing (defined as Orders III to XVI of the 1958 (Revised) Standard Industrial Classification). In the Census tabulations it is grouped with employment in construction (Order XVII) and gas, water, electricity undertakings (Order XVIII) but these other classes account for only 99,000 employees in the Conurbation (81,000 in construction) compared with 696,000 in manufacturing. The proportion of Conurbation workers in manufacturing was 54·2 per cent in 1966, compared with only 34·2 per cent in England and Wales as a whole. In the city of Birmingham, 52·2 per cent of its workers were in manufacturing in 1966, still high but less than the Conurbation average, indicating the city's wider service base as the regional capital. These figures, from the published tables of the census, are for the proportions of jobs available, not for the employment of residents. In the maps, the type of employment is shown by the place of residence of workers. They do not show the actual location of manufacturing jobs. We know that there is a high degree of commuting movement within the Conurbation, so that any correspondence between the patterns of employment on the computer maps and the locations of job opportunities, in the major industrial areas and the town and city centres (see endpapers), cannot be investigated in detail. Many workers, especially office workers and skilled manufacturing workers, travel considerable distances to other parts of the Conurbation to work. There is also a considerable movement into the Conurbation from outside, as we have already noted in the Introduction. Nevertheless, for the Conurbation as a whole, it may be assumed that the majority prefer to work relatively near home, if suitable job opportunities are available. In a major industrial region of the scale and complexity of the West Midlands Conurbation, these opportunities are, of course, often available.

Even more characteristic of the West Midlands, of course, is the area's specialization in the metal industries. The metal industry groups (1958 Standard Industrial Classification Orders V, metal manufacture; VI, engineering and electrical goods; VIII, vehicles; and IX, metal goods) account for no less than 43·4 per cent of all employment in the Conurbation and 40·7 per cent in Birmingham, compared with only 17·7 per cent for England and Wales. There is some difference of emphasis between the two halves of the Conurbation: for instance, the heavier foundry industry is found in the Black Country, while lighter forms of metal processing and assembly are predominant in Birmingham, but the metal, engineering and vehicle specializations are of universal importance.

The detailed figures used in preparing these two maps show that in 1966 no ward had less than 41 per cent of its residents working in manufacturing, construction and public utilities, and the maximum was 81 per cent. In Birmingham the range of enumeration districts was from 27 per cent to 83 per cent. The Conurbation map shows very clearly how important these groups are in the Black Country. A north–south belt, where more than 71 per cent of the economically active residents work in manufacturing, stands out. It includes such areas (from north to south) as Willenhall, Bilston, Darlaston, Wednesbury, Tipton, the western areas of West Bromwich, extending south-westwards to Dudley and Brierley Hill. In comparison, only the Aston–Witton area, to the north of Birmingham city centre is so dependent upon manufacturing. There is no doubt that the central and north Birmingham area is the most important single industrial area of the Conurbation, but the proximity of the city centre, with other types of employment for local residents, and the large number of people who travel from other areas to work in this industrial zone, reduces the dependence of Birmingham people upon manufacturing.

The north to south zone in the Black Country marks the most characteristic industrial 'con-urban' area of the West Midlands forming a string of communities with housing and industry closely intermixed both physically, economically and socially. The larger, more self-contained towns like Wolverhampton and Walsall are still important manufacturing centres, like Birmingham (with 55–60 per cent of residents in manufacturing), but their inhabitants are able to find more service jobs, either locally or, through better transport facilities, in other centres. Generally speaking, the location of workers in distribution and other services forms a pattern that

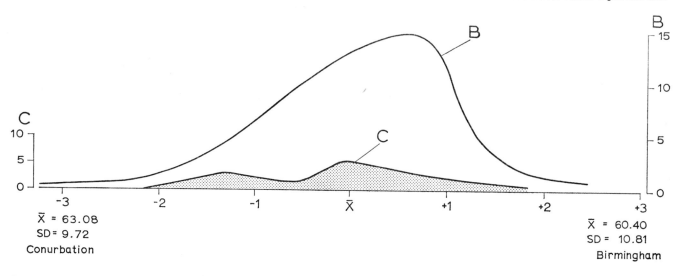

C

10
5
0

−3   −2   −1   X̄   +1   +2   +3

X̄ = 63.08
SD = 9.72
Conurbation

B
15
10
5
0

X̄ = 60.40
SD = 10.81
Birmingham

is the complement of this. The areas where they are most significant and where manufacturing is least important (less than 46 per cent in manufacturing) are, of course such places as Solihull, Sutton Coldfield, parts of south-west Birmingham and the areas of similar socio–economic character on the west of the Conurbation.

The pattern of manufacturing employment in Birmingham is, as with many of the variables studied in the atlas, much more detailed and complex. Still, it can be related to housing areas and their associated social classes on the one hand and to the distribution of industrial areas on the other. For historical reasons, of course, these are by no means independent of each other. Generally, in the central part of the city, there is a clear relationship between more than about 69 per cent of workers in manufacturing and areas of high-density housing (see endpapers, right). In the suburbs, in Kingstanding on the north, at Castle Bromwich and Stechford on the east, at Acocks Green to the south-east, Kings Norton on the south and Longbridge in the south-west, pockets of manufacturing employment are associated with industrial concentrations, even though many workers in these areas must also travel to other industrial areas in the city. The next lower level of representation (greater than 62 per cent) shows much

broader zones, especially in the central and northern areas of Birmingham and in the south-west, emphasizing the low belt of Edgbaston–Moseley–Yardley Wood, already referred to (variable 3). The major nodes are in an arc around the north of the city centre from Ladywood on the west, through Winson Green to Aston, Saltley and Balsall Heath on the south-east of the city centre. The land-use map (endpapers, right) indicates that the radiating sectors of manufacturing that have grown up since the First War to the north of the city centre (Witton and along Tyburn Road to the north-east) and to the south-west (Sparkbrook to Acocks Green) have a very marked effect in raising the level of manufacturing employment in adjacent housing areas, as well as attracting large numbers from other parts of the city.

The strongest correlations with this widespread characteristic are negative, particularly with professional, managerial and government occupations (variables 7 and 28). More interesting correlations are with areas containing high proportions of unskilled workers (variable 6), small dwellings (variable 16), family sharing of households (variable 8, particularly the Black Country,) low car ownership (variable 3) and council renting (variable 14).

Conurbation

Variable	Stepwise multiple correlation	Simple correlation
7 Professional and managerial group	·78	−·78
21 Irish immigrants	·83	(not significant)
23 Sex ratio	·84	−·40
8 Households with 2+ families	·85	·60
4 Married women working	·86	·47
27 Distribution workers		−·97
6 Unskilled group		·66
16 Dwelling size		−·65
3 Cars per household		−·59
14 Council renting		·56
42 Persons per room		·53
28 Governmental workers		−·52
17 Migration into local authority		−·50
4 Married women working		·47
19 Multiple dwellings converted		−·46
37 Skilled workers		·46
34 Female employment		·45

Birmingham

Variable	Stepwise multiple correlation	Simple correlation
7 Professional and managerial group	·69	−·69
27 Distribution workers		−·95
6 Unskilled group		·56
3 Cars per household		−·49
42 Persons per room		·43
2 Outside w c		·41
28 Governmental workers		−·40
30 Travel to work		·40

Variables 27, Distribution workers and 28, Governmental workers have been eliminated from the multiple correlation matrix because of multicollinearity.

Source: 1966 Census Ward Data, Base Map prepared by The Centre for Urban and Regional Studies, University of Birmingham

6 Conurbation The percentage of the economically active and retired males who are in the unskilled socio–economic groupings

Maximum included in highest level only

1	2	3	4	5	6	7	8
5·00–10·00	10·00–15·00	15·00–20·00	20·00–25·00	25·00–30·00	30·00–35·00	35·00–40·00	40·00–45·00

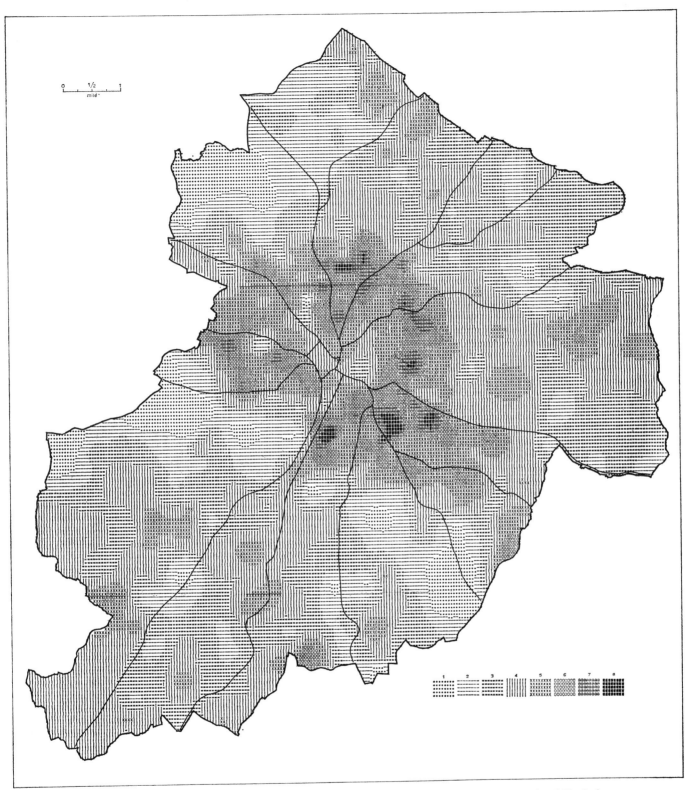

Source: 1966 Enumeration-District Data, Base Map prepared by The Centre for Urban and Regional Studies, University of Birmingham

6 Birmingham The percentage of the economically active and retired males who are in the unskilled socio–economic groupings

Maximum included in highest level only

1	2	3	4	5	6	7	8
5·00–12·00	12·00–19·00	19·00–26·00	26·00–33·00	33·00–40·00	40·00–47·00	47·00–54·00	54·00–61·00

Variable 6

The percentage of the economically active and retired males in the unskilled socio–economic groupings

In variable 5, manufacturing employment was distinguished according to a classification of the types of activity in which people work. Other categories in this classification used in the analysis, although the maps are not included in the atlas, group together 'distribution and civilian service' workers (variable 27) and 'government' employees (variable 28). The 'unskilled' groups shown here, like those classified as professional and managerial workers under variable 7, arise from the *socio–economic* classification used in the census. This attempts to group together males whose social, cultural and recreational standards and behaviour are similar (see *Classification of Occupations*, H.M.S.O., 1966). In fact the census does not ask direct questions about individual standards or behaviour so that the classification is simply based upon employment status and occupation, with an implicit assumption that the various groups are relatively homogeneous in their ways of life.

This variable traces the proportions of economically active and retired males who are in socio–economic groupings 7, 10, 11 and 15, semi-skilled and unskilled manual workers and personal service workers. These groups contain workers with the lowest economic potential of the various socio–economic categories in the Conurbation. The shortage of labour prevalent recently has meant that many of them have obtained continuous work and fairly good wages. In times of recession, however, it is these groups that are the first to be laid off and there is always a seasonal fluctuation in the demand for poorly qualified workers, especially in the construction industry. In the longer term, of course, automation and the reorganization of industrial methods in the region is likely to make some semi-skilled and unskilled workers redundant, although of course skilled manual workers, with their specialized training, may also be vulnerable in certain cases. Unemployment rates in the Conurbation have generally been very low in the post-war period but the rise in recent years has impinged upon these groups most directly.

In the Conurbation wards, the range of values for this variable is from 5 to 45 per cent of the economically active males. The frequency distribution is near normal, with a slight positive skew (i.e. with more wards with less than the median value of 25 per cent). In the city of Birmingham, the range in enumeration districts is from 5 to 61 per cent

and here the distribution is very near to normal around the median value of 33 per cent. The Conurbation map shows the relative preponderance of these workers in the central areas of Birmingham compared with the rest of the Conurbation. Large parts around the centre of the city have more than 35 per cent of male workers in unskilled categories when measured by wards. The broader zone of unskilled workers in the Conurbation, with more than 25 per cent of economically active males in these categories, follows a south-east to north-west trend, stretching through the centre of the Conurbation from Birmingham to Wolverhampton, via Smethwick, Dudley, Wednesbury and Bilston. Another zone runs at right angles to this axis, from Aldridge in the north through Walsall, to Dudley and Brierley Hill in the south. Particularly high concentrations are found near to the centres of the major towns, such as Wolverhampton, Walsall, Bilston and Smethwick. This pattern is not very closely related to that of manufacturing employment (variable 5). It follows much more closely the areas of poor housing and environmental conditions traced in Sections I and V.

In Birmingham the major concentrations of unskilled workers are in the inner wards of the city, both in the areas now undergoing redevelopment and in the generally poor housing around them. The association, discussed under variable 2, of poor housing and the poor economic position of its inhabitants is unmistakable, especially in such areas as Aston, to the north of the city centre, Washwood Heath and Bordesley Green, to the east, Small Heath and Sparkbrook to the south-east, Balsall Heath to the south and Ladywood to the west. Elsewhere in the city there are no strong concentrations of unskilled workers. Areas of council housing (variable 14), for example, appear to have hardly more unskilled workers than other areas. The Edgbaston–Moseley belt to the south-west of the city, which we will see is strongly represented with professional and managerial groups, stands out as particularly low, as do the areas of Handsworth Wood and Quinton on the north-west and south-west borders of the city.

In the Conurbation this index shows many strong correlations with other variables. The strongest are negative, with areas having high proportions of cars per household (variable 3) and owner-occupied tenancy (variable 13). Areas with many unskilled workers also have a high use of public transport to work (variable 30) and lack basic amenities such as inside w.c.s (variable 2) and hot water (variable 32). They also score high

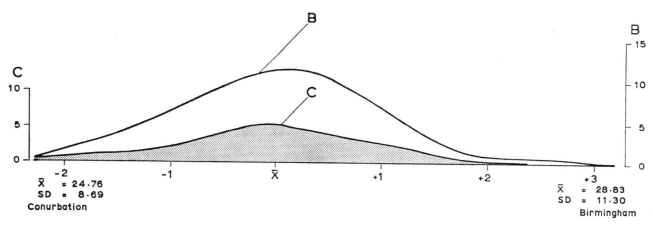

X̄ = 24·76
SD = 8·69
Conurbation

X̄ = 28·83
SD = 11·30
Birmingham

in manufacturing employment (variable 5) and with the overcrowding index (variable 39, proportion of households living at more than 1½ persons per room). At the Conurbation level, there is a strong negative association between areas of unskilled occupations and recent movement into new local authority areas to live (variable 17). Most families who have done this are headed by professional and service workers and have taken up residence on the Conurbation periphery. Other significant correlations include those with the proportion of households with no family (variable 29, single persons living alone), the percentage of women working (variable 34), households with two or more families (variable 8), council-rented dwellings (variable 14) and unemployment (variable 41). In Birmingham much the same variables are related significantly to the proportion of unskilled workers, although in a somewhat different order. Areas of relatively high immigrant representation (Irish and New Commonwealth, variables 21 and 22) are only weakly related to the distribution of unskilled workers as defined here.

The location of unskilled workers throughout the Conurbation is thus closely related to poor housing conditions; in these areas rehabilitation and redevelopment is thus an economic and social problem as well as one for the planners of physical housing developments.

Conurbation

Variable	Stepwise multiple correlation	Simple correlation
3 Cars per household	·84	—·84
13 Owner-occupied	·92	—·80
22 New Commonwealth immigrants	·93	·49
7 Professional and managerial group		—·84
30 Travel to work		·74
2 Outside wc		·70
27 Distribution workers		—·69
5 Manufacturing workers		·66
39 Households occupied 1½+ persons per room		·64
42 Persons per room		·64
32 Lacking hot water		·63
17 Migration into local authority		—·62
29 Households without families		·60
34 Female employment		·59
8 Households with 2+ families		·57
14 Council renting		·57
41 Unemployment rate		·53
36 2-person households		·52
35 Sharing sink and stove		·51

Birmingham

Variable	Stepwise multiple correlation	Simple correlation
30 Travel to work	·61	·61
5 Manufacturing workers	·70	·56
13 Owner-occupied	·74	—·52
22 New Commonwealth immigrants	·80	·48
3 Cars per household	·80	—·57
23 Sex ratio	·83	—·41
7 Professional and managerial group		—·67
37 Skilled workers		—·56
27 Distribution workers		—·55
32 Lacking hot water		·52
39 Households occupied 1½+ persons per room		·51
2 Outside wc		·51
21 Irish immigrants		·42
24 Fertility ratio		·42

Variables 7, Professional and managerial group and 37, Skilled workers have been eliminated from the multiple correlation matrix because of multicollinearity.

Source: 1966 Census Ward Data, Base Map prepared by The Centre for Urban and Regional Studies, University of Birmingham

7 Conurbation The percentage of the economically active and retired males who are in the professional and managerial socio–economic groupings

Maximum included in highest level only

1	2	3	4	5	6	7	8
2·00–8·00	8·00–14·00	14·00–20·00	20·00–26·00	26·00–32·00	32·00–38·00	38·00–44·00	44·00–50·00

Source: 1966 Enumeration-District Data, Base Map prepared by The Centre for Urban and Regional Studies, University of Birmingham

7 Birmingham The percentage of the economically active and retired males who are in the professional and managerial socio–economic groupings

Maximum included in highest level only

1	2	3	4	5	6	7	8
0·00–5·00	5·00–10·00	10·00–15·00	15·00–20·00	20·00–25·00	25·00–30·00	30·00–35·00	35·00–40·00

Variable 7

The percentage of the economically active and retired males in the professional and managerial socio–economic groupings

The professional and managerial groups shown here, like those classified as unskilled workers under variable 6, arise from the *socio–economic* classification used in the census. The socio–economic groups that are mapped include numbers 1, 2, 3, 4 and 13. Groups 1 and 2 are employers and managers in government, industry and commerce; groups 3 and 4 are professional workers, generally defined as requiring qualifications of at least university first degree standard, whether working for themselves or as employees; and group 13 includes farmers and so can be assumed to be unimportant in this study. Other socio–economic groups include such categories as foremen, skilled manual workers, workers on their own account, non-manual workers and the unskilled workers whose patterns of location in the Conurbation have already been examined, in variable 6.

The range of ward values in the Conurbation is large, from 2 per cent to 50 per cent and the frequency distribution is highly skewed, many wards having very low representations. The same feature is found in Birmingham, where the general level of representation is lower and the enumeration-district range is from 0 to 40 per cent.

Undoubtedly, this variable unambiguously represents the higher paid, high prestige groups in the Conurbation and they most consistently occupy Sutton Coldfield in the north-east, Solihull in the south-east and the Pedmore area of Stourbridge in the south-west. In these areas the principal wards have more than 35 per cent of males in these socio–economic groupings. Other areas, such as Great Barr in the north, Halesowen in the south and Tettenhall and parts of southern Wolverhampton on the west of the Conurbation, have more than 25 per cent representation.

In Birmingham, large parts of the city have very small proportions of these groups, in common with other areas of the Conurbation. The average representation in 1966 was 9·9

per cent but the great majority of enumeration districts had a lesser proportion than this. The tendency for this type of worker to move to peripheral areas has extended, as we saw in the Conurbation map, beyond the boundaries of the city. Many of the managerial and professional workers in Birmingham factories and offices live in Solihull, Sutton Coldfield and even farther afield in the Green Belt villages and towns. The same feature applies to these classes of workers in the Black Country. In the city, however, certain sectors of the suburbs still house concentrations of these high income groups. The main areas are to the south of the city centre, in the north-west to south-east zone through Edgbaston, Moseley and Hall Green. This forms a consistent belt, of high cost, low-density housing, broken only by the lines of the main roads. The land-use map shows this belt of low-density housing quite clearly (endpapers, right) and in these areas more than 35 per cent of the males were in the professional and managerial groups in 1966. The Edgbaston part of this area originally developed in the early decades of the nineteenth century as a suburb selected to house the rich men of the city and their families. It retained this character until the Second World War and has been undergoing redevelopment in more recent years, under the control of the Calthorpe Estate Company, the principal leaseholder. This redevelopment is intended to retain the low-density, residential character of most areas of Edgbaston (see Reference 28). Moseley and Hall Green were built at a later date so that there has been a lesser problem of redevelopment so far. Handsworth Wood, in the north-west of the city provides another area of similar character, with high income groups in large houses at low densities per acre, built between the two World Wars. In the south-west of the city, parts of Northfield, Kings Norton and Kings Heath also have considerable proportions of professional and managerial workers, mostly in houses built during the past fifty years.

The patterns on this map do not follow any form of concentric pattern, determined by phases of the city's growth.

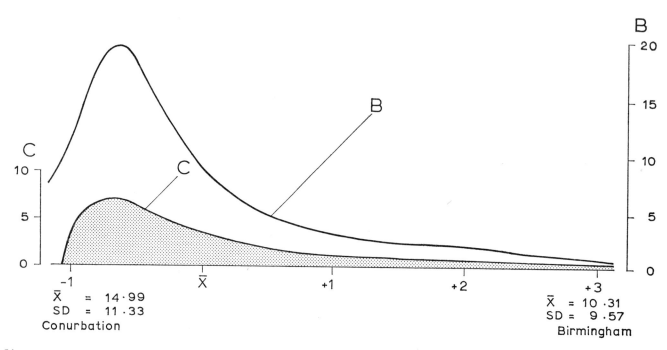

X̄ = 14·99
SD = 11·33
Conurbation

X̄ = 10·31
SD = 9·57
Birmingham

The distributions of some variables shown in the atlas do suggest that perhaps the long-established age divisions between inner, middle and outer rings have an effect upon the social character of different areas (see particularly the maps of the age structure of the population in Section III). Here, the patterns of high income groups forms a number of nodes in certain sectors of the city which have been segregated as élite areas through several phases of urban growth.

Today, even though the principal belt of concentration for this variable has retained its special character, changes have taken place in the occupational structure of its inhabitants; they are less frequently in the managerial groups than formerly (nowadays these more commonly live outside the city) and more often in the professions. The area has also been quite markedly affected by the rapid growth of the university in Edgbaston in recent years.

The correlation analysis confirms the geographical association of special characteristics that would be expected for high income and prestige groups; high car ownership (variable 3), large, owner-occupied houses (variables 13 and 16) and high proportions of residents who have recently moved into the area from other local authorities (variable 17). The last variable is strongly associated with professional and managerial groups in the Conurbation as a whole, reflecting movement to Sutton Coldfield and Solihull, but is not significant for the city of Birmingham. Certain other types of worker, employed in service industries (variable 27) and national and local government (variable 28), are also found in the same areas in higher than average proportions. Other aspects of the areas that emerge strongly on the maps of this variable will appear in Section IV of the atlas, where several of the highly correlated variables mentioned above will be examined in detail.

Conurbation		
Variable	Stepwise multiple correlation	Simple correlation
27 Distribution workers	·82	·82
3 Cars per household	·91	·82
17 Migration into local authority	·94	·72
16 Dwelling size	·95	·66
6 Unskilled group		—·84
13 Owner-occupied		·78
5 Manufacturing workers		—·77
42 Persons per room		—·66
14 Council renting		—·64
34 Female employment		—·60
30 Travel to work		—·58
37 Skilled workers		—·58
8 Households with 2+ families		—·58
2 Outside wc		—·53
36 2-person households		—·49
4 Married women working		—·43
32 Lacking hot water		—·41
28 Government workers		·41

Birmingham		
Variable	Stepwise multiple correlation	Simple correlation
27 Distribution workers	·71	·71
13 Owner-occupied	·78	·53
3 Cars per household	·82	·56
5 Manufacturing workers		—·69
6 Unskilled group		—·66
42 Persons per room		—·51
30 Travel to work		—·44
14 Council renting		—·44
2 Outside wc		—·48
16 Dwelling size		·40

Variables 37, Skilled workers and 6, Unskilled group have been eliminated from the multiple correlation matrix because of multicollinearity.

1 2 3 4 5 6 7 8

Source: 1966 Census Ward Data, Base Map prepared by The Centre for Urban and Regional Studies, University of Birmingham

8 Conurbation The percentage of households with 2 or more families

Maximum included in highest level only

1	2	3	4	5	6	7	8
0·0–0·80	0·80–1·60	1·60–2·40	2·40–3·20	3·20–4·00	4·00–4·80	4·80–5·60	5·60–6·40

Source: 1966 Enumeration-District Data, Base Map prepared by The Centre for Urban and Regional Studies, University of Birmingham

8 Birmingham The percentage of households with 2 or more families

Maximum included in highest level only

1	2	3	4	5	6	6	8
0·0–1·50	1·50–3·00	3·00–4·50	4·50–6·00	6·00–7·50	7·50–9·00	9·00–10·50	10·50–12·00

Variable 8

The percentage of households with two or more families

This index, although at first sight rather a curious one to choose for particular study, demonstrates an interesting and distinctive pattern within the Conurbation. It hints at a feature of the social geography of the region that is not represented in any of the other maps in this atlas. The census definitions need to be kept in mind in considering the patterns of these maps (See Introduction). The term 'household' implies generally a common housekeeping. A 'family' consists technically of married couples, with or without their never married child or children. Individual parents living with their never married children and grandparents living with their never married grandchildren are also included. 'Children' in this context may include 'in-law', 'step' and 'adopted' relationships but not foster relationships. Thus, when households with two or more families are being considered, the most commonly recognized situation is where older married or widowed relatives live with their married children or grandchildren (i.e. 'living with "in-laws"'). A lodger, like all single persons does not constitute a separate family within the household, although an unrelated married couple, with or without children, does so. Thus we have here an index of the adequacy of the housing stock in each area to fulfil its family needs and also, if regarded in another way, a measure of residential cohesiveness between different generations within the extended family.

The highest values plotted on the maps are not very great, of course. In the Conurbation wards, the range is from 0 to 6·4 per cent of the households having two or more families and in the Birmingham enumeration districts it is from 0 to 12·0 per cent. In both cases, the distribution is positively skewed but in the Conurbation the modal values are in the 1·6 to 2·4 per cent octile division while in Birmingham the lowest division, from 0 to 1·5 per cent has the largest number of enumeration districts within it. A glance at the Conurbation map reveals the most important geographical fact about this measure: it is tracing a predominantly Black Country feature. Considerable areas of the central Black Country have more than 4·8 per cent of their households shared between families. The Birmingham half of the Conurbation has no wards that achieve this level of household sharing. The principal areas are in Tipton, Bilston, Darlaston, the Upper Gornal area of Dudley C.B., and the industrial belt running from West Bromwich in the south, east of central Wednesbury, to southern Walsall on the north. Most of these areas form part of the typically amorphous industrial–residential sprawl of the Black Country. The more general zone, which excludes the major peripheral towns, might almost be taken to define the social and environmental 'problem area' of the old industrial Conurbation. Even in Birmingham, it is the more industrial, working-class areas of the northern part of the city that have relatively high proportions of households shared by families. The detailed map of the city adds little apart from this general emphasis on the northern areas. Individual nodes indicate high values for enumeration districts that cannot be accepted as statistically significant. There are no consistent zones with more than the median value of representation.

In the Conurbation as whole, the correlation analysis indicates a number of interesting associations with this variable. The primary correlation concerns the industrial structure of employment in the areas where household sharing is found; employment in manufacturing (variable 5) is most common.

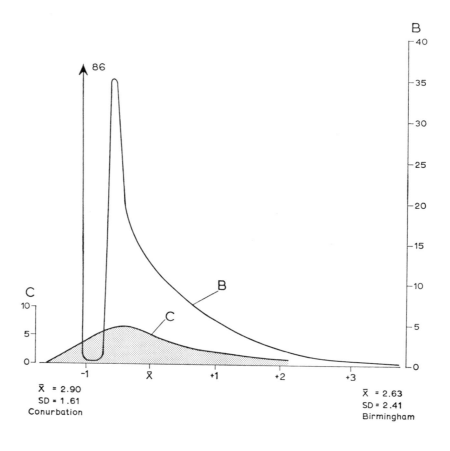

$\bar{X}$ = 2.90
SD = 1.61
Conurbation

$\bar{X}$ = 2.63
SD = 2.41
Birmingham

Of equal importance is household tenure; areas with high proportions of council housing (variable 14) in the Black Country most commonly have high degrees of sharing between families. Other significant correlations are with unskilled workers (variable 6), and with high average numbers of persons per room (variable 42), as might be expected. Another significant correlation is negative; the proportion of the population that had moved into the local authority during the five years before the census (variable 17). In other words, family sharing of households is not a characteristic of groups moving to the newer housing areas on the edge of the Conurbation, but one of the 'stable' population of the old Conurbation, at least as measured by this mobility index. In the city of Birmingham, as might be expected from what has already been said, there are no very significant correlations; no suggestion of consistent traits within the city that produce family sharing.

The association of the geographical patterns with characteristics such as manufacturing employment, council house tenure, unskilled workers and relative locational stability in the population suggests that the form of over-crowding traced in this variable is rather different from that traced, for example, in Section V. It is tempting to suggest that this variable plots the geographical incidence of 'traditional' social cohesiveness within the industrial parts of the Black Country. Certainly, it is the strongest index of the distinctiveness of these areas that has emerged from this census analysis. It also identifies areas of social distress, however. The sharing of households by different generations was mentioned in the Introduction as a problem that would impinge upon planning policy in the region over the next twenty years. These maps indicate where this feature is most concentrated and, while many of the housing problems of the Conurbation have been generated by the overcrowded city of Birmingham, it is clear from these maps that this problem is characteristically a result of overcrowding in the Black Country.

Conurbation

Variable	Stepwise multiple correlation	Simple correlation
13 Owner-occupied	·64	—·64
5 Manufacturing workers	·69	·60
14 Council renting		·59
27 Distribution workers		—·58
6 Unskilled group		·57
7 Professional and managerial group		—·56
42 Persons per room		·53
17 Migration into local authority		—·52
3 Cars per household		—·47
36 2-person households		·42
16 Dwelling size		—·42
34 Female employment		·41

Birmingham

Variable	Stepwise multiple correlation	Simple correlation
7 Professional and managerial group	·26	—·26
34 Female employment	·33	·23
16 Dwelling size	·38	(not significant)
14 Council renting	·44	·22
13 Owner-occupied		·25
27 Distribution workers		—·25
6 Unskilled group		·23
5 Manufacturing workers		·23

III Age Structure

Source: 1966 Census Ward Data, Base Map prepared by The Centre for Urban and Regional Studies, University of Birmingham

Section III Conurbation factor 3 Age Structure

Factor score, maximum included in highest level only

1	2	3	4	5	6	7	8
4·25–5·50	3·00–4·25	1·75–3·00	0·50–1·75	−0·75–0·50	−2·00–−0·75	−3·25–−2·00	−4·50–−3·25

Not altogether unexpectedly, the variables that group themselves into this factor do not exhibit the highest powers of differentiation between areas within either the whole Conurbation or the city of Birmingham. In the former area they constitute the third most important factor, after the divisions according to 'affluence' (Section I) and housing tenure (Section IV) have been accounted for. In Birmingham, they form only the fifth factor, of very little value at the local scale of analysis employed in studying the city. The factor includes various measures of the age structure of the Conurbation's population which, of course, is affected by many other aspects of its social, economic and geographical structure, discussed in other sections.

Nevertheless, demographic measures are fundamental to an understanding of the variable character of urban areas and, in the generalized analysis of the whole Conurbation (based upon wards), this is the main factor that relates to the population, as opposed to the measures of dwelling character found in factors 1 and 2 (Sections I and IV). At this scale, the factor map for the Conurbation distinguishes broad zones of relatively homogeneous age structure and, to state the major distinction in its most general form, separates areas of old aged population (dark) from younger areas (light). The 'old' areas have high proportions of people in the 45–64 and over 64 age groups and, naturally very low proportions of children (0–14 year olds). They are also associated in the factor with high proportions of working women, and, to a lesser extent, of working men and high proportions of two-person families. All of these attributes, of course, are inverted in the 'young' areas; we are not solely concerned with age structure in considering this factor, therefore, but also with associated employment characteristics and family size.

The details and significance of these patterns will be discussed in more detail when we deal with the individual age groups. Areas of larger families and lower proportions of women working are, however, found mainly on the periphery of the Conurbation; on the north, in a continuous zone from north Wolverhampton and Wednesfield, through north Walsall and including all of Aldridge and Brownhills, with the outer parts of Sutton Coldfield. The southern boundary is less consistent but Solihull, south-western Birmingham and southern Stourbridge again have high proportions of young families. A young population is found only around Kingswinford and Sedgley on the western edge of the Black Country, both areas of extensive recent house building. Within the main built-up area, the most outstanding area of young families is found in the central wards of Birmingham and the nearby parts of Smethwick. The northern parts of West Bromwich, where recent housing has taken place, also forms an embayment into the heart of the Black Country.

The areas of older population form a marked ring around central Birmingham, in the well-established suburbs of the city, extending northwards into Sutton Coldfield and westwards into the complex pattern of the Black Country. This centres particularly upon the Willenhall–Walsall area in the north and the Brierley Hill–Halesowen area on the south. The significance of these zones in relation to the evolving planning problems of the Conurbation will be discussed in more detail when we present the maps of the individual variables. This section presents the three most important age groups: 0–14, 45–64 and over 64 years old, and also the related measure of male activity rates (proportion of males in the 15–64 age groups at work). The very important problem of female activity rates has already been considered in Section I, in discussing the proportion of married women working (variable 4).

Conurbation factor 3			Other high factor loading		
Variable	Factor loading	Commun-ality	Section	Factor	Factor loading
9 Age 0–14*	·933	·935			
26 Dependency ratio*	·931	·943			
10 Age 45–64*	−·856	·781			
11 Age 65+*	−·792	·868	I	1	·396
40 Economically active*	−·703	·870	II	5	−·518
			I	1	−·303
36 2-person households	−·697	·757	IV	2	−·385
34 Female employment*	−·614	·765	IV	2	−·414
			II	5	−·390
24 Fertility ratio	·588	·826	I	1	·658
42 Persons per room	·457	·935	IV	2	·457
			II	5	−·472
12 Male employment*	−·409	·368	II	5	−·304

Birmingham factor 5			Other high factor loading		
Variable	Factor loading	Commun-ality	Section	Factor	Factor loading
26 Dependency ratio*	·802	·884	I	3	−·397
			II	1	·353
9 Age 0–14*	·710	·846	I	3	−·342
			IV	4	·318
34 Female employment*	−·697	·570			
40 Economically active	−·674	·789	I	3	·564
36 2-person households*	−·634	·216			
10 Age 45–64*	−·583	·670	V	2	·362
24 Fertility ratio	·496	·702	IV	4	−·520
11 Age 65+	·478	·615	II	1	−·457
42 Persons per room	·370	·819	IV	4	·565
			II	1	·551
12 Male employment*	−·270	·205	V	2	·247

* Principal variables in this factor.

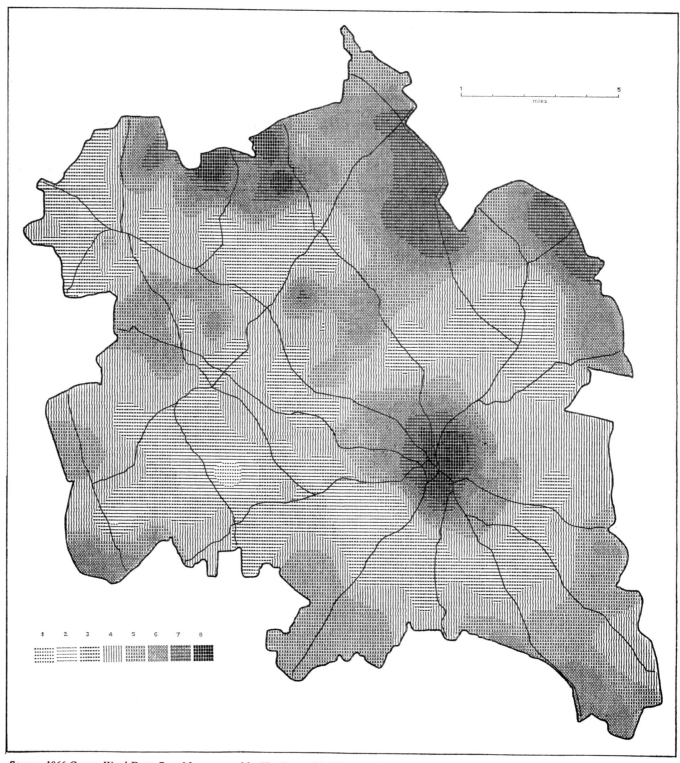

Source: 1966 Census Ward Data, Base Map prepared by The Centre for Urban and Regional Studies, University of Birmingham

9 Conurbation The percentage of the total population aged 0–14

Maximum included in highest level only

1	2	3	4	5	6	7	8
14·00–16·50	16·50–19·00	19·00–21·50	21·50–24·00	24·00–26·50	26·50–29·00	29·00–31·50	31·50–34·00

Source: 1966 Enumeration-District Data, Base Map prepared by The Centre for Urban and Regional Studies, University of Birmingham

9 Birmingham The percentage of the total population aged 0–14

Maximum included in highest level only

1	2	3	4	5	6	7	8
9·00–14·00	14·00–19·00	19·00–24·00	24·00–29·00	29·00–34·00	34·00–39·00	39·00–44·00	44·00–49·00

Variable 9

The percentage of the total population aged 0–14

The age structure of the population, indicated here by certain key age groups, is a variable that must be perpetually anticipated in planning. The population 'pyramid' of any area evolves through various stages as time passes and also, at any particular moment, will differ from area to area. These variations are of great significance in assessing the social needs and economic capabilities of different places. For example, housing estates built during the 1930s were first occupied mainly by young families – the houses were predominantly built for this purpose. At that time, therefore, it was important to provide infant and junior schools and medical services which could deal with pre- and ante-natal problems and with the illnesses of children. Today, over thirty years later, these areas are relatively weighted in their age structures towards the middle-aged and elderly, although many of the original inhabitants may have retired elsewhere to be replaced by young families. A balance of age groups may come about after two or three generations but, for the present, medical services may have a disproportionate need to cater for older people.

This example indicates how new housing areas proceed through phases of development towards a relatively 'balanced' age structure. Nevertheless, the age structure of some areas may be permanently affected by the nature of their housing stock; for example, estates of small privately owned family houses will tend to be renewed with young families fairly regularly from generation to generation. Larger houses, on the other hand, or blocks of flats tend to be occupied more by middle-aged people, often in professional and managerial jobs.

A particular example of houses affecting the age characteristics of their occupants rather less directly, although no less effectively, is found in slum areas. Whether they are 'old' working-class slums or the more recently developed areas of subdivided late nineteenth-century housing, today these tend to accommodate young families and large numbers of children. The main reason for this is that these areas suffer a high 'turnover' of occupants compared with standard suburban housing areas: out of preference or necessity many families do not stay in a particular slum house for long, especially in

rented rooms, in subdivided houses. In the current period of acute housing shortage in our large cities and of high private housing costs, young families on low incomes tend to be funnelled into this available cheap slum accommodation. This is particularly so if they have recently migrated from another part of the country or from abroad, so that they do not qualify for council housing (more will be said about this in Section V).

The distinction between privately owned and council housing may also affect the age structure of an area, since people living in the latter are generally less able to move away as they grow older and their need for family housing diminishes. Better provision of smaller dwellings for middle-aged and elderly people by local councils may reduce this differential in the future.

The youngest age groups, analysed through this variable, are distributed in a manner that well illustrates several of these general points. The child population of the Conurbation was only slightly more predominant than the average for England and Wales in 1966 comprising 23·6 per cent of the total population, compared with 23·0 per cent and the city of Birmingham had virtually the same proportion. The range of values in the wards of the Conurbation is from 14 per cent to 34 per cent and in the enumeration districts of Birmingham, from 9 to 49 per cent. As with each of the age-structure variables, the frequency distribution is near normal but with a slight positive skew (the category of values with the largest number of areas is below the middle value of the range).

As might be expected from the previous remarks, the areas with high proportions of children in the **Conurbation** have a marked dichotomy of socio–economic character. Areas with more than 31·5 per cent of their populations in the 0–14 age groups were found in the central wards of Birmingham, in the north-east part of Sutton Coldfield and in the Bloxwich–Wednesfield area in the north of the Black Country. The first of these is clearly an area of poor slum housing while the other areas were rapidly developed in the early 1960s as new housing areas, both privately built and of council housing, for young families. Other areas with high proportions of children (more than 26·5 per cent) included Aldridge, with extensions to Great Barr and West Bromwich and, in the south, the

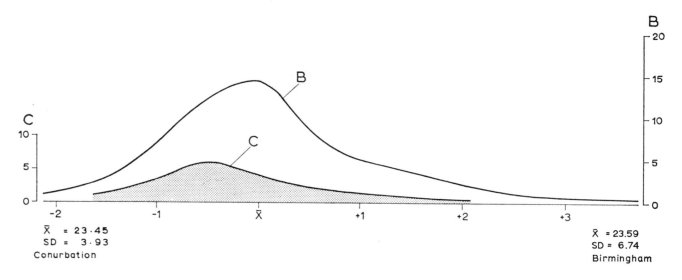

X̄ = 23·45
SD = 3·93
Conurbation

X̄ = 23.59
SD = 6.74
Birmingham

southern fringes of Stourbridge and Solihull. These are largely areas of private housing development for relatively well-off young families.

In Birmingham, the familiar circle of slum houses around the city centre emerges from the detailed map, including Ladywood, southern Aston, Saltley and Balsall Heath. Redevelopment is changing this area radically although it is likely that a young age structure will be retained, at least for the present generation. In the suburban areas, places such as Bartley Green and parts of Longbridge and Kings Norton stand out in the south-west, where new estates have been built in recent years. Elsewhere, no really consistent patterns emerge except for an area with relatively few children in a north to south belt through Edgbaston, Selly Oak and Bournville and also extending to the east, through Moseley and Hall Green.

The correlation analysis matches this variable with such obviously related indices as the dependency ratio (variable 26, children and unemployed women divided by the number of workers), low proportions of other age groups (variables 10 and 11), high fertility (variable 24, children aged 0–4 divided by the number of women aged between 15 and 45) and low proportions of economically active persons (variable 40). More interesting correlations emerge from the detailed

analysis of Birmingham, where indices of poor housing, such as a lack of hot water and inside w.c.s (variables 2 and 32) and overcrowding (variable 39, high proportions living at more than $1\frac{1}{2}$ persons per room) are also important. In Birmingham, it is clear that the worst housing areas have high proportions of young people.

The principal significance of these geographical distributions is for the problems of social, medical and especially educational provision. The acute problems of the poorest parts of Birmingham, which are traced in Section I and were also noted in discussing variable 6, unskilled workers, are accentuated once again by population pressure on inadequate schools. In the near future, these areas will be in urgent need of youth services and other policies to anticipate problems in the teenage groups. In certain sectors of the Conurbation periphery, educational developments are also of considerable current importance as a result of the age structure. The problems in these areas are not, however, compounded by the other ills found around the centre of the Birmingham. Elsewhere, educational facilities may be more adequate, at least in simple numerical terms. In fact, in the areas that we will now consider, such facilities may even be in surfeit.

Conurbation

Variable	Stepwise multiple correlation	Simple correlation
40 Economically active	·65	−·65
4 Married women working	·87	(not significant)
42 Persons per room	·93	·63
36 2-person households	·94	−·56
12 Male employment	·96	(not significant)
26 Dependency ratio		·90
10 Age 45–64		−·84
11 Age 65+		−·72
24 Fertility ratio		·60
39 Households occupied $1\frac{1}{2}$+ persons per room		·32

Birmingham

Variable	Stepwise multiple correlation	Simple correlation
42 Persons per room	·64	·64
40 Economically active	·80	−·61
12 Male employment	·83	(not significant)
4 Married women working	·88	(not significant)
36 2-person households	·90	−·33
2 Outside wc	·91	·46
26 Dependency ratio		·86
10 Age 45–64		−·74
24 Fertility ratio		·71
32 Lacking hot water		·57
11 Age 65+		−·51
39 Households occupied $1\frac{1}{2}$+ persons per room		·46

Variables 26, Dependency ratio, 24, Fertility ratio, 10, Age 45–64, and 11, Age 65+, have been eliminated from the multiple correlation matrix because of multicollinearity.

Source: 1966 Census Ward Data, Base Map prepared by the Centre for Urban and Regional Studies, University of Birmingham

10 Conurbation The percentage of the total population aged 45–64

Maximum included in highest level only

1	2	3	4	5	6	7	8
15·00–17·25	17·25–19·50	19·50–21·75	21·75–24·00	24·00–26·25	26·25–28·50	28·50–30·75	30·75–33·00

Source: 1966 Enumeration-District Data, Base Map prepared by The Centre for Urban and Regional Studies, University of Birmingham

10 Birmingham The percentage of the total population aged 45–64

Maximum included in highest level only

1	2	3	4	5	6	7	8
10·00–14·00	14·00–18·00	18·00–22·00	22·00–26·00	26·00–30·00	30·00–34·00	34·00–38·00	38·00–42·00

Variable 10

The percentage of the total population aged 45–64

The significance of areas with high proportions of young and old people (0–14 and over 64 years old) has already been suggested in discussing the last variable. These extreme age groups have a particular importance that makes their examination worthwhile. In the maps of areas with high proportions of children, distinct patterns were evident and the character and problems of the various areas could be relatively easily summarized. As we shall see, the distribution of old people (over 64 years), although less clear-cut than the pattern of youth also has certain areas of marked concentration. In demonstrating the distribution of the 45–64 year olds, we should not expect such concentrations or any simple patterns of distribution. And yet this age group has perhaps a more long-term and subtle significance for the social geography of the Conurbation. For, while the other age groups presented in this section represent current 'problem areas' of one kind or another, the 'middle-aged' groups offer both a reflection of the social history of the last generation and an anticipation of future changes. Most of the suburbs that stand out on the maps of this variable were established in the pre-war period. They retain a characteristic age structure in spite of considerable changes since then. These are the areas of established and relatively stable population at present that will in future face the problems of ageing and change now arising in the areas shown by the next variable. If we can regard our cities and conurbations as changing systems of activity, one of the basic variables in assessing the contribution of each area is age structure; young and old areas are centres of change in the economic and social structure of the city but the middle-aged areas shown here are the relatively stable units. In spite of a preoccupation with the dynamics of change, it is important to account for stability and inertia in the urban system.

The average representation of these age groups in England and Wales was 25·1 per cent in 1966. This proportion was very closely reflected in the Conurbation but Birmingham has a slightly older population, with 25·5 per cent in the middle-aged groups and also a higher than average proportion in the over 64 group (see next variable). The variations between

Conurbation wards was from 15 to 33 per cent while, in Birmingham, the enumeration-district values range from 10 to 42 per cent.

The distribution in the Conurbation is, to some extent, the inverse of the pattern for the 0–14 age group shown by the last variable. Certainly, the central areas of Birmingham and the northern areas of the Conurbation, which stand out so clearly on the maps of that variable, have very low values here. The most consistent feature of the pattern, which is otherwise rather haphazard, is the broad belt of suburban Birmingham, where proportions are consistently higher than 26 per cent and in many areas greater than 28·5 per cent. This belt extends into Sutton Coldfield on the north of the city and into Smethwick on the west. All of these areas also have a high proportion of persons over 64 years of age (see next variable). Almost as a continuation of this belt, West Bromwich, Halesowen, Cradley Heath, Dudley and Brierley Hill form a marked group of areas in the southern half of the Black Country. In the north there is another area of marked concentration, around Willenhall and Wednesbury. These are the demographically and socially more stable areas of the Black Country. Significantly, the rather less aggressively industrialized areas of the Black Country, in its southern half, appear to be more prominent. The other areas with high representations of these age groups are rather different in character, being located in relatively peripheral locations. Like Sutton Coldfield, already mentioned, Solihull on the south-east of the Conurbation and the areas to the west of Wolverhampton form well-established satellite communities for the middle-aged middle classes.

In Birmingham, the enumeration-district map of these age groups shows the stable elements in the social geography of the city, in contrast to the central areas traced by the last variable and the areas of potential change to be discussed next. In the north the Handsworth Wood–Kingstanding area forms the most prominent single block with considerable areas having more than 34 per cent of residents in this category. On the east there is a zone from Castle Bromwich and Stechford to Sheldon, generally with more than 30 per cent, although with certain nodes of higher values and, in the south-

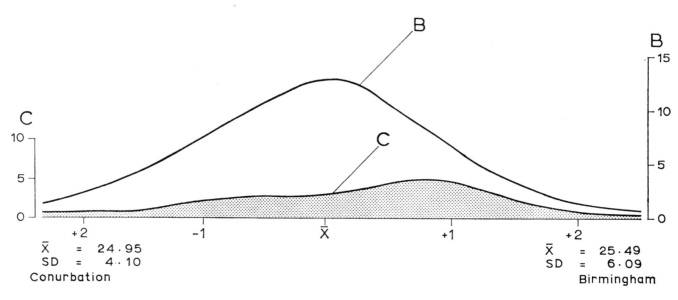

X̄ = 24·95
SD = 4·10
Conurbation

X̄ = 25·49
SD = 6·09
Birmingham

east, the Hall Green–Yardley Wood area has a similar character. In the south-western part of the city, the areas of interwar housing in the Harborne–Weoley Castle–Quinton areas are prominent. As with the Conurbation at large, the main zones of low values correspond to the areas with high proportions of under 14 years olds. Certain of the more recently built housing areas in the suburbs also have poor representations of the middle-aged, however: for example on the eastern fringes of the city, at Bartley Green on the south-west, and in the Moseley area, south of the city centre.

The correlation analysis does not draw out many associations, as might be expected with such a socially and economically ubiquitous variable as middle age. There is a strong positive association, as has already been mentioned, with the older

age group, over 64 years old, and the areas where the middle age groups are important also have high proportions of both men and women working (variables 40 and 34) coupled with small proportions of young children (variable 9) and low average numbers of person per room (variable 42).

In the Introduction to this atlas, some mention was made of the 'intermediate' areas of the Conurbation which are neither the problem areas of its centre nor the rapidly growing sectors on its periphery. This variable plots this intermediate belt as well as any other. The areas traced here are important for planning because, as the maturity of the population increases in spite of some people moving away to retire, they will become distinctively old-aged in their character and social needs.

Conurbation

Variable	Stepwise mutliple correlation	Simple correlation
26 Dependency ratio	−·75	−·75
4 Married women working	·80	(not significant)
24 Fertility ratio	·84	−·56
9 Age 0–14		−·84
11 Age 65+		·64
40 Economically active		·52
36 2-person households		·49
42 Persons per room		−·48
34 Female employment		·40

Birmingham

Variable	Stepwise multiple correlation	Simple correlation
26 Dependency ratio	·67	−·67
18 Households sharing dwellings	·76	−·38
34 Female employment	·78	·26
23 Sex ratio	·79	(not significant)
17 Migration into local authority	·80	−·31
9 Age 0–14		−·74
42 Persons per room		−·55
40 Economically active		·54
39 Households occupied 1½+ persons per room		−·54
24 Fertility ratio		−·54
32 Lacking hot water		−·43
21 Irish immigrants		−·42

Variables 9, Age 0–14 and 11, Age 65+ have been eliminated from the multiple correlation matrix because of multicollinearity.

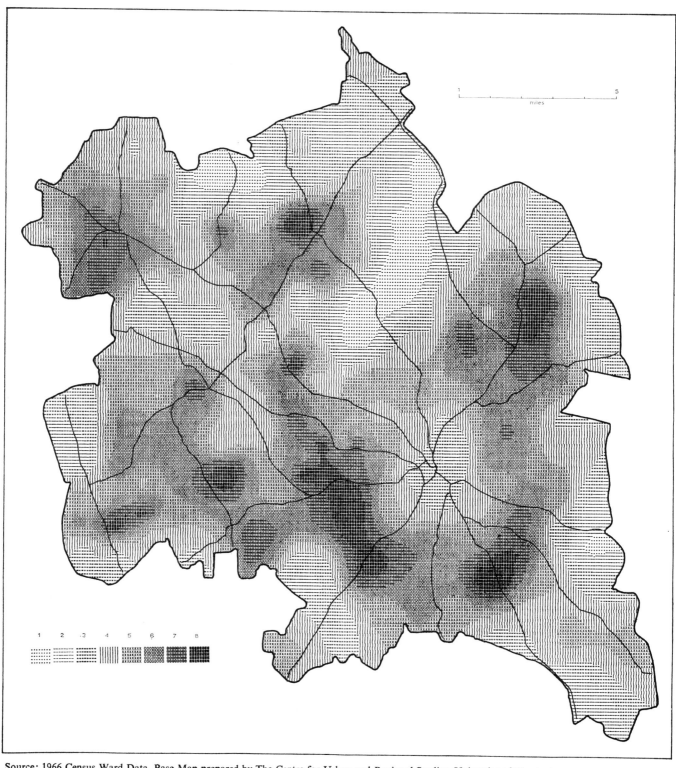

Source: 1966 Census Ward Data, Base Map prepared by The Centre for Urban and Regional Studies, University of Birmingham

11 Conurbation The percentage of the total population that is older than 64 years

Maximum included in highest level only

1	2	3	4	5	6	7	8
4·00–5·50	5·50–7·00	7·00–8·50	8·50–10·00	10·00–11·50	11·50–13·00	13·00–14·50	14·50–16·00

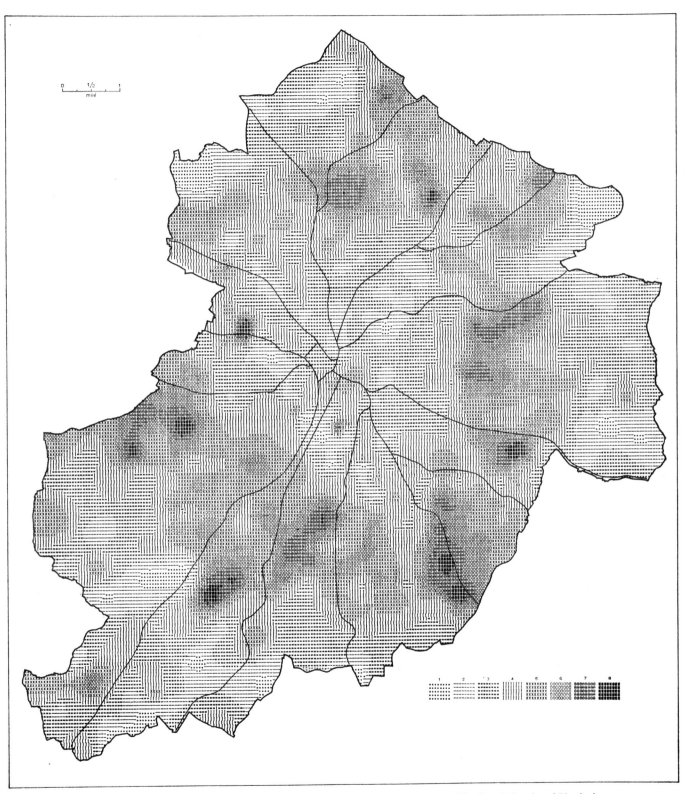

Source: 1966 Enumeration-District Data, Base Map prepared by The Centre for Urban and Regional Studies, University of Birmingham

11 Birmingham The percentage of the total population that is older than 64 years

Maximum included in highest level only

1	2	3	4	5	6	7	8
1·00–4·00	4·00–7·00	7·00–10·00	10·00–13·00	13·00–16·00	16·00–19·00	19·00–22·00	22·00–25·00

Variable 11

The percentage of the total population older than 64 years

The significance of areas with high proportions of old people for planning and for the provision of suitable amenities has already been suggested. The social and demographic history of certain areas gives their age structure a particular emphasis upon the elderly, even though all areas have some proportion of residents in each age group. Thus in the Conurbation in 1966, the average proportion of persons over 64 years of age was 10·3 per cent, exactly the same as the figure for England and Wales. The proportion in Birmingham was slightly higher, at 10·8 per cent. In the Conurbation, the range of values for wards was from 4 per cent to 16 per cent and in Birmingham, the enumeration-district values were, as usual, more extreme, from 0 to 25 per cent. Thus, even in the enumeration district that had the highest proportion, old people accounted for only one quarter of the residents and it would be misleading to speak of areas with relatively high proportions of people over 64 as if they were geriatric ghettos. It would also be misleading to imply that the particular needs of old people should be provided for in these high areas and neglected elsewhere; the degree of segregation is generally quite low.

Nevertheless, the maps of the last variable combined with these indicate that substantial proportions of the Conurbation have a markedly old-aged structure. There is a significant correspondence between areas with high proportions of over 64 years old and those with high proportions of 45–64 years (variable 10). In the case of the last variable, we were examining the stable elements of the populations in 1966. Here, inevitably, we are examining the element on the population that is most likely to change in the next ten years. In the same manner as in other areas in the recent past, the passing of an old generation may cause important social changes where it is particularly strongly represented. Even though only 15 to 20 per cent of the resident population of certain areas is involved, a turnover of population of this scale within a ten-year period is considerable in its effects on the character of an area.

In the Conurbation, the areas where persons over 64 are particularly important (over 13 per cent of the resident population), include a group of Birmingham suburbs similar to those outlined in the last section. Again, the inner areas of the city

and the outer suburbs clearly favour younger families. Sutton Coldfield also appears important once more, unlike Solihull with which it is often compared. Although Solihull has some concentration of the 45–64 age groups, as we saw in discussing the last variable, Sutton Coldfield is clearly the older established of the two main satellites of Birmingham. In the Black Country, nodes of relatively old population structure are found around the centres of the main towns: Walsall and Willenhall in the north, West Bromwich and Dudley in the central area and Stourbridge, Cradley Heath and Halesowen on the south. This simple association between the central areas of Black Country towns and old age contrasts, of course, with the pattern for Birmingham, where the central areas are young. The contrast may be more apparent than real, however, as a result of the size of the wards around these centres in relation to the size of towns. More detailed, enumeration-district analysis of these 'local' patterns would be needed to confirm the existence of this contrast. One exception to this rule in the Black Country is found in Smethwick, where the emphasis upon old people is found in the interwar housing estates west of Smethwick, forming an apparent continuation of the Edgbaston–Harborne belt in south-west Birmingham. Another exception occurs in Wolverhampton, where the main areas of old people are found south of the town centre, rather than around the centre itself.

The enumeration-district map of Birmingham provides a detailed anatomy of the 'belt of old age' in the intermediate suburbs of the city. It is similar in form to that described for the 45–64 age group under variable 10, but excludes some of the outer suburbs, particularly on the east and north of the city, that are included there. The belt includes parts of Perry Barr and Witton on the north of the city; parts of Kingstanding, Short Heath and Erdington on the north-east; a zone from Stechford, through Yardley to Acocks Green on the east and a marked node in Hall Green, along the Stratford Road on the south-east. The most consistent zone of old age, however, stretches across the south and south-west of the city, including Moseley and Kings Heath, the Bournville estates (which stand out very markedly), and much of Edgbaston and Harborne in the south-west sector. Substantial areas of all these suburbs had more than 13 per cent of their residents over 64 years old in 1966.

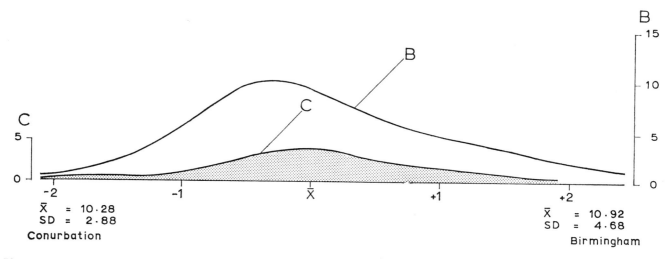

$\bar{X}$ = 10·28
SD = 2·88
Conurbation

$\bar{X}$ = 10·92
SD = 4·68
Birmingham

72

As might be expected from the example of the two age groups already discussed, correlations of other distributions with the areas where old people live are not very strong – old age is a fairly common constituent of the population. In the Conurbation at large, a significant association is noted with the 45–64 age groups (variable 10) and with the proportion of women of working age who actually work (variable 34). Two-person households (variable 36) are understandably important in the same areas as old people and privately rented dwellings (variable 20) also emerge as significantly correlated. Negative associations reveal that old-aged areas have low proportions of married women working (variable 4, this index includes the over 64 year old, of course) and low average numbers of persons per room (variable 42); the inverse of overcrowding. In Birmingham, the correlations are few and negative; most significantly with the proportion of married women working (variable 4) and the average number of persons per room (variable 42).

These correlations confirm the image of areas with high proportions of old people, rather than providing additional information about the distribution of this age group. As has been suggested, however, it is unlikely that other socio-economic variables would be strongly associated with such an age group variable.

Conurbation

Variable	Stepwise multiple correlation	Simple correlation
26 Dependency ratio	·65	−·65
40 Economically active	·92	(not significant)
34 Female employment	·95	·45
23 Sex ratio	·97	·34
9 Age 0–14		−·72
10 Age 45–64		·64
36 2-person households		·61
29 Households without families		·55
20 Private renting		·47
4 Married women working		−·46
42 Persons per room		−·45
34 Female employment		·45
1 All basic amenities		−·38
3 Cars per household		−·32

Birmingham

Variable	Stepwise multiple correlation	Simple correlation
42 Persons per room	·53	−·53
4 Married women working	·64	−·44
34 Females employed	·74	·22
9 Age 0–14		−·51
23 Sex ratio		·37
36 2-person households		·35
26 Dependency ratio		−·32
10 Age 45–64		·28
5 Manufacturing workers		−·28
27 Distribution workers		·28

Variables 9, Age 0–14, and 10, Age 45–64 have been eliminated from the multiple correlation matrix because of multicollinearity.

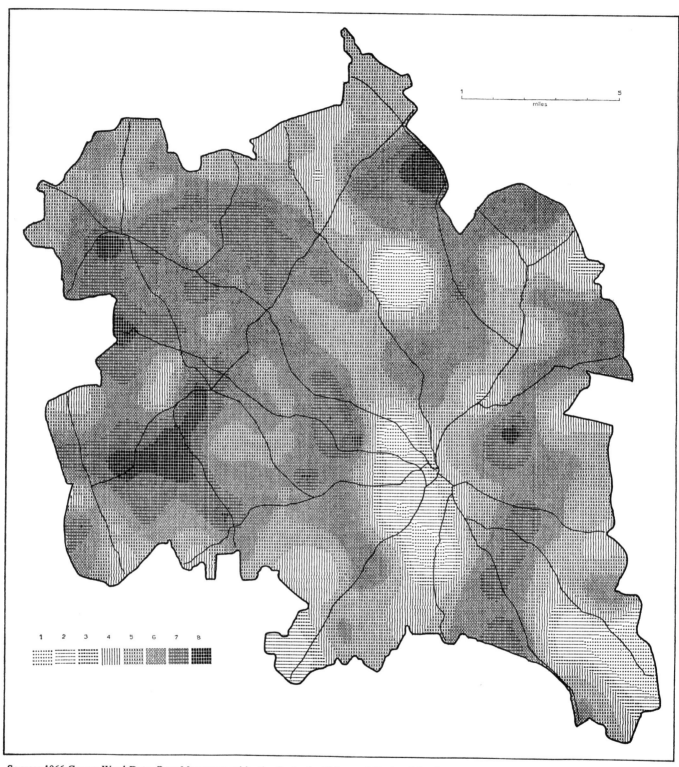

Source: 1966 Census Ward Data, Base Map prepared by the Centre for Urban and Regional Studies, University of Birmingham

12 Conurbation The proportion of males aged 15–64 who are working

Maximum included in highest level only

1	2	3	4	5	6	7	8
89·00–90·50	90·50–92·00	92·00–93·50	93·50–95·00	95·00–96·50	96·50–98·00	98·00–99·50	99·50–101·00

Source: 1966 Enumeration-District Data, Base Map prepared by The Centre for Urban and Regional Studies, University of Birmingham

12 Birmingham The proportion of males aged 15–64 who are working

Maximum included in highest level only

1	2	3	4	5	6	7	8
75·00–80·00	80·00–85·00	85·00–90·00	90·00–95·00	95·00–100·00	100·00–105·00	105·00–110·00	110·00–115·00

Variable 12

The proportion of males aged 15–64 working

The maximum working life of a male in this country is generally accepted to be from the end of compulsory school attendance, at 15, to the standard age of retirement, 65 years. Male activity rates are therefore normally related to this age span; here the numbers of working males resident in each area are compared in percentage terms with the numbers living there aged 15–64. We have already seen (variable 4) that female activity rates vary widely from place to place in response to an apparently complex set of socio–economic variables. Generally, however, men have to work and their activity rates are normally around 100.

The detailed causes of the variations in male activity rates are seldom clear, mainly because there are at least two sets of influences at work. The main general reason for differences from place to place is related to the proportion of teenagers who stay at school after 15 and receive full-time education, perhaps up to the age of 21. This participation in full-time education to various ages after 15 is, of course, an increasingly important trend today but it is affected in its geographical incidence by two local conditions. First, the age structure of the population; if there are relatively large proportions in the 15–21 age group, a larger proportion of the potential male workers are likely to be receiving further education. Conversely, if the emphasis in the general male population is towards older age groups within the 15–64 range (see variable 10), the proportion at work will generally be higher. Secondly, the social structure of areas is likely to influence male activity rates. This is because full-time further education is generally pursued less by teenagers from industrial working-class families than by those from 'white collar' middle-class families. Working-class areas might therefore be expected to have higher male activity rates. National statistics for participation in further education suggest that the West Midlands has one of the lowest rates in the country (see Reference 14). The emphasis upon manufacturing industry in the region, together with its high prosperity and wage levels, provides a general explanation. A good deal of further education and training in the region takes place, however, on a part-time basis and much, of course, is in the form of apprenticeships and other types of training at work.

From these observations it is to be expected that areas of middle and old-aged, working-class population in the Conurbation are likely to have the highest activity rates, while areas with young–middle aged, middle-class families are likely to have the lowest. Other combinations are possible, however: housing estates that have recently been occupied by couples in their twenties with young children would have high rates; older middle-class areas might have low rates because of another important trend – early retirement. On the other hand, such locally or personally important conditions as unemployment or disablement are not general enough in the West Midlands to provide any explanation for our mapped patterns. Another important feature that emerges from an examination of these two maps is the obvious tendency within the West Midlands Conurbation to stay on at work after the accepted retirement age. The demand for skilled workers in particular keeps older men at work in large numbers and the ranges of values plotted from the census data confirms this.

Even allowing for the reasons that have been discussed for activity rates to fall below 100, the maximum ward value in the Conurbation for this variable was 101 in 1966. The minimum value in the range was 89·0. In the enumeration-district analysis of Birmingham the range was much greater, as might be expected, with a maximum of 115·0 and a minimum of 75·0. The pattern of incidence in the Conurbation map confirms in a general manner the contrasts outlined above. High areas (greater than 98) are generally the old and middle-aged working-class suburbs of Birmingham, on the east of the city (compare with variables 10 and 11) and the older parts of the northern and southern Black Country (southern Walsall–Willenhall–Wednesfield, and Dudley–Cradley Heath–Brierley Hill–Halesowen). Other areas that stand out, however, such as a large node in Aldridge, eastern Sutton Coldfield and the Sedgley–southern Wolverhampton area of the western Black Country are very different in character, being mainly occupied by young families in new housing estates. The areas of low

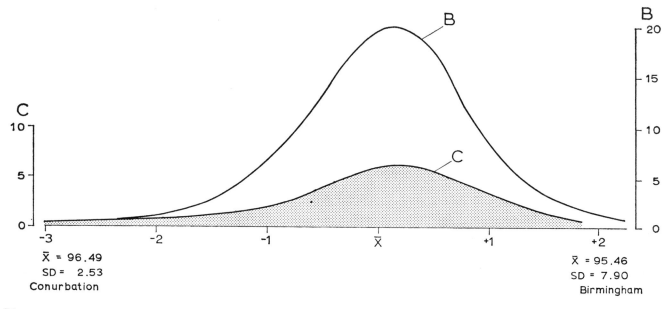

X̄ = 96.49
SD = 2.53
Conurbation

X̄ = 95.46
SD = 7.90
Birmingham

activity rates are found, as might be expected, in the middle-class satellite town of Solihull (but not the older centre of Sutton Coldfield), and the generally middle-class suburbs of southern Birmingham. The most extreme areas of low values, however, are probably accounted for by the large number of students in the various educational institutions of this part of the city. The area also contains a considerable hospital population and this feature probably explains the extremely low values in the Great Barr area.

In Birmingham, the enumeration-district map confirms the importance of low activity rates (less than 90) in the Edgbaston–Moseley belt and in other middle-class suburbs such as Harborne, Quinton, Northfield, parts of Longbridge and Kings Norton on the south-west, and in the eastern suburbs, from Shard End to Sheldon. Nearer the centre of the city an apparently very varied pattern is found. Unfortunately, the 10 per cent sample enumeration-district data cannot be relied upon for a pattern of this complexity. The Ladywood–Winson Green area to the west of the city centre is particularly complex because of its concentration of hospital and prison institutions.

The complexity that lies behind this index is confirmed by the correlation analysis, which also, it will be recalled, was of very little aid in discussing married female activity rates in variable 4. In the Conurbation a significant, although low negative correlation is suggested between wards with low activity rates and those with high numbers of dependants (mainly children) per worker (variable 26). In Birmingham there appears to be some correlation between enumeration districts with low activity rates and unemployment (variable 41).

The variety of influences at work in producing this pattern of male activity rates has been described, if not fully analysed. The manner in which the variable falls into this section in the factor analysis suggests that age structure provides the most satisfactory general basis upon which to discuss male activity rates, although we have seen how other factors modify its influence to a considerable degree.

Conurbation

Variable	Stepwise multiple correlation	Simple correlation
26 Dependency ratio	·37	−·37
21 Irish immigrants	·48	−·34
9 Age 0–14	·56	−·25
40 Economically active		·36
11 Age 65+		·29
5 Manufacturing workers		·29
36 2-person households		·29

Birmingham

Variable	Stepwise multiple correlation	Simple correlation
41 Unemployment rate	·47	−·47
3 Cars per household	·51	(not significant)
40 Economically active	·57	·35
20 Private renting	·60	−·19
26 Dependency ratio		−·24
34 Female employment		·22
37 Skilled group		·22

Source: 1966 Census Ward Data, Base Map prepared by The Centre for Urban and Regional Studies, University of Birmingham

Section IV Conurbation factor 2 Housing Tenure

Factor score, maximum included in highest level only

1	2	3	4	5	6	7	8
7·00–5·50	4·00–5·50	2·50–4·00	1·00–2·50	−0·50–1·00	−2·00–−0·50	−3·50–−2·00	−5·00–−3·50

Section I was concerned with the varying quality of dwellings and other indices that appear to be associated with this. It was clear that, at the Conurbation scale of ward analysis, the difference between housing with and without basic amenities provides the primary distinction traced by the census within the built-up area. The variables of this section group themselves into the second factor in the analysis of the Conurbation data. They form the second most powerful basis for distinguishing between the character of areas in the Conurbation, after the 'affluence' measures of Section I. In the enumeration-district analysis of Birmingham, however, they are of subsidiary importance, forming only the fourth factor, after employment (Section II), the 'zone of transition' measures (Section V) and relative 'affluence' (Section I).

The distinctive properties that give high scores for this factor to certain areas in the Conurbation (and, inversely, are absent from low areas) may best be summarized with reference to its two major variables: the proportion of dwellings that are rented from local authorities and the proportion that are owner-occupied. Housing tenure, therefore, seems to provide the key distinction within this factor, augmenting the patterns of housing quality that we have seen in Section I. The other variables in this factor elaborate this near dichotomy: the areas with high proportions of council-rented property are also associated with migration within the respective local authority areas, rather than into the areas from outside, with small dwellings, with purpose-built blocks of flats and maisonettes ('multiple dwellings', in census jargon) and with higher than average numbers of persons per room. In addition, these areas also have a relatively high use of public transport for travelling to work in the Conurbation, although this feature does not emerge clearly in the analysis of Birmingham.

Although many areas have only either council houses or privately owned houses, this distinction is complicated elsewhere in the Conurbation by a third type of tenure: renting of dwellings from private landlords. The occurrence of this variable is traced in detail in Section V, since it has a parti-cular significance for the 'zone of transition' which appears in the enumeration-district analysis of Birmingham. In terms of the factor which forms the basis of this section, however, areas of privately rented dwellings clearly have closer affinities with areas of privately owned houses than with those of council-rented property (i.e. in their attraction of migrants from outside the local authority, their larger dwellings size, lack of purpose-built blocks of multiple dwellings, etc.).

The factor map for the Conurbation shows, in dark shading, areas which possess the combination of characteristics associated with council renting that we have listed for this factor. The Black Country half of the Conurbation stands out clearly, particularly the northern part, from Wednesfield to Bloxwich, around Bilston, Wednesbury and West Bromwich, with extensions southwards to the east and west of central Dudley. Areas of similar dwelling character occur on the eastern borders of Birmingham and also in the south-west of the city.

Opposite characteristics are found in such, by now familiar, peripheral areas of the Conurbation as Sutton Coldfield, Solihull, Halesowen, Stourbridge and western Wolverhampton. Large areas of the middle suburbs of Birmingham, with extensions into Smethwick also have very low scores for this factor and here the influence of privately rented dwellings is very marked in providing the contrast with publicly owned areas.

The variables that we have presented in this section include both of the 'primary' variables, the proportions of owner-occupied and council-rented dwellings; also, the proportion of purpose-built blocks of dwellings, indicating the effect of one of the most significant trends in recent house building; average dwelling size; and the proportions of the population that have moved into the local authority area within the previous five years. The last variable is more related to areas of privately rented property and thus to the 'zone of transition' in the city of Birmingham (Section V), but, as we have seen, is closely associated with areas of high owner-occupation at the scale of the whole Conurbation.

Conurbation factor 2			Other high factor loading		
Variable	Factor loading	Commun-ality	Section	Factor	Factor loading
13 Owner-occupied*	·822	·901	I	5	·413
14 Council renting*	−·822	·897	II	5	−·331
17 Migration into local authority	·730	·767	III II	3 5	·329 ·312
42 Persons per room*	−·704	·935	II III	5 3	−·472 ·457
25 Mobility within area*	−·690	·590	V	4	·316
24 Fertility ratio	·658	·826	III	3	·588
16 Dwelling size*	·602	·861	I	5	·534
30 Travel to work	−·533	·795	I	1	·585
15 Multiple dwellings purpose-built*	−·532	·363			
6 Unskilled group	−·521	·888	II I	5 1	−·574 ·467
7 Professional and managerial group	·518	·879	II	5	·736
8 Households with 2+ families	−·443	·470	II	5	−·485
34 Female employment	−·414	·765	III II	3 5	−·614 −·390
11 Age 65+	·396	·868	III	3	−·792

Birmingham factor 4			Other high factor loading		
Variable	Factor loading	Commun-ality	Section	Factor	Factor loading
13 Owner-occupied*	−·801	·888	I	1	−·338
14 Council renting*	·795	·856	V	2	·340
15 Multiple dwelling purpose-built*	·694	·639			
25 Mobility within area*	·634	·441			
42 Persons per room*	·565	·819	II III	1 5	·551 ·370
20 Dwelling size*	−·550	·724	V	2	−·592
24 Fertility ratio	−·520	·702	III	5	·496
11 Age 65+	−·457	·615	III	5	·478

* Principal variables in this factor

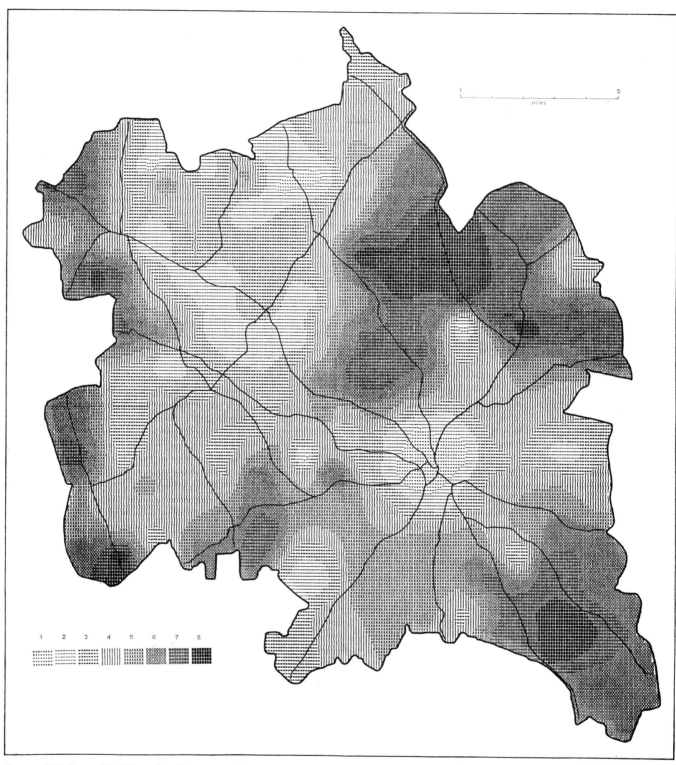

Source: 1966 Census Ward Data, Base Map prepared by The Centre for Urban and Regional Studies, University of Birmingham

13 Conurbation The percentage of dwellings that are owner-occupied

Maximum included in highest level only

1	2	3	4	5	6	7	8
0·00–11·50	11·50–23·00	23·00–34·50	34·50–46·00	46·00–57·50	57·50–69·00	69·00–80·50	80·50–92·00

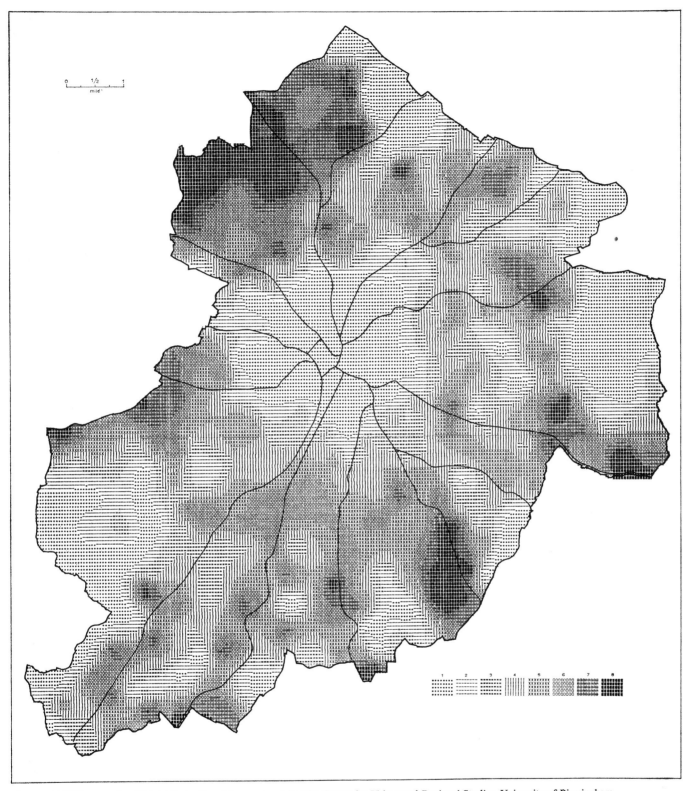

Source: 1966 Enumeration-District Data, Base Map prepared by The Centre for Urban and Regional Studies, University of Birmingham

13 Birmingham The percentage of dwellings that are owner occupied

Maximum included in highest level

1	2	3	4	5	6	7	8
0·00–12·00	12·00–24·00	24·00–36·00	36·00–48·00	48·00–60·00	60·00–72·00	72·00–84·00	84·00–96·00

The percentage of dwellings owner-occupied

The most common type of tenure in Britain is freehold owner-occupation (including houses in course of purchase by mortgage). For the purposes of the census classification, dwellings occupied on a lease granted for at least 21 years, either originally or by later extension, are also counted in this category. In 1966, 48·7 per cent of private dwellings in England and Wales (including flats and maisonettes) were owner-occupied or held on a long lease. The West Midlands Conurbation had 43·0 per cent of its dwellings in this class and Birmingham had only 39·9 per cent. The occurrence of this type of tenure within any urban area in this country has a wide range of values, however, and this is the basis of the very important distinction in British cities between areas of privately owned and rented property. Thus in the West Midlands Conurbation, the percentage of dwellings that is owner-occupied, by wards, ranges from 0 to 92. For the city of Birmingham the enumeration-district values exhibit a range from 0–96 per cent.

This segregation of the two main types of tenure broadly corresponds to the ownership of land and the original agency of house building, whether private or public. The principal distinction is between privately owned housing and publicly owned, rented accommodation, although some areas have important sectors of privately rented property. The parallel economic and social distinctions are also important, even though they may be more intangible. Our analysis throws some light upon these, within the limitations of the census data.

In the **Conurbation**, high owner-occupation is found in the areas that have already been pointed out for their high rates of car ownership (variable 3) and their socio–economic specialization into the professional and managerial groups (variable 7). Solihull and Sutton Coldfield (except for an area of council housing on the east of the latter) stand out and, to the west of Sutton, the Streetly–Great Barr–Handsworth area is also prominent once more. In relation to these, the city of Birmingham, as the average statistics already quoted would suggest, has a generally low representation of owner-occupied

houses (less than 50 per cent). Much of the Black Country is also very sparsely provided for and it is clear that the average picture for the Conurbation is heavily weighted by the Sutton Coldfield and Solihull areas. Only wards in the western suburbs of Wolverhampton and Brierley Hill and in the southern parts of Stourbridge and Halesowen have similar proportions of owner-occupied housing.

Quite large areas of the central Conurbation have less than 23 per cent of their dwellings in this type of tenure, which obviously forms an important constituent of the housing problem in these old areas. They are being deserted by young families wishing to purchase their own homes. The low areas in the Conurbation are predominantly occupied by council housing, except for the wards of central Birmingham, Smethwick, Walsall and Wolverhampton, where private renting is more important (variable 20).

In Birmingham, the frequency distribution of this variable is strongly skewed, indicating the large number of enumeration districts with very little privately owned housing, in council estates and in the areas of privately rented accommodation. The marked difference between the histograms for the Conurbation and Birmingham results from the different scale of analysis between wards and enumeration districts. This becomes significant when a locally segragated variable such as housing tenure is being considered (as opposed to variables that show segregation on the scale of the whole Conurbation, such as in Section I).

In Birmingham, areas of Erdington and Castle Bromwich in the north-east had more than 60 per cent of their dwellings owner-occupied in 1966 as did parts of Yardley and Sheldon in the east. Much of the southern part of the city also had extensive areas with more than 60 per cent of privately owned housing, especially in Hall Green, Moseley, Kings Heath and around Kings Norton and Northfield. On the west the area of Harborne, Quinton and western Edgbaston stand out clearly but the largest area of owner occupied housing is in the north-west; in Handsworth, Handsworth Wood and western Kingstanding. The more recent private house building has taken place nearer to the outskirts of the city, especially on the south (see next variable).

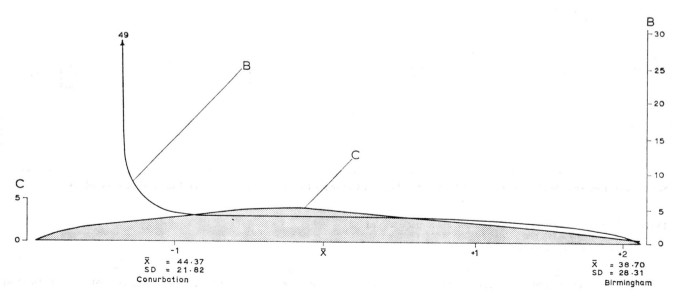

X̄ = 44.37
SD = 21.82
Conurbation

X̄ = 38.70
SD = 28.31
Birmingham

The correlation analysis relates the distribution of high owner-occupation very strongly to that of professional, managerial and service workers (variables 7, 27). Dwelling size (variable 16) is also significantly related to this type of tenure as well as the ownership of cars (variable 3) and their use in travelling to work (variable 30). As might be expected from what has already been said (variable 6), the proportion of unskilled workers is negatively related to owner-occupation,

as is the persons per room index of relative overcrowding (variable 39). Families that have recently moved into local authority areas from outside (variable 17) are found in areas with high proportions of privately owned houses in the Conurbation at large, although this does not seem to apply to Birmingham, where shortage of housing has directed most recent immigrants to areas where privately renting is more common than average (variable 20).

Conurbation

Variable	Stepwise multiple correlation	Simple correlation
6 Unskilled group	·80	— ·80
16 Dwelling size	·87	·68
29 Households without families	·90	— ·45
1 All basic amenities	·92	(not significant)
2 Outside wc	·98	— ·58
14 Council renting		— ·90
7 Professional and managerial group		·78
42 Persons per room		— ·76
17 Migration into local authority		·75
27 Distribution workers		·65
8 Households with 2+ families		— ·64
5 Manufacturing workers		— ·62
30 Travel to work		— ·60
3 Cars per household		·59
36 2-person households		— ·55
34 Female employment		— ·54
25 Mobility within area		— ·54
39 Households occupied 1½+ persons per room		— ·47
32 Lacking hot water		— ·42
41 Unemployment rate		— ·40

Birmingham

Variable	Stepwise multiple correlation	Simple correlation
42 Persons per room	·59	— ·59
36 2-person households	·73	— ·38
16 Dwelling size	·80	·56
29 Households without families	·85	— ·35
33 Sharing wc	·87	(not significant)
17 Migration into local authority	·88	·31
15 Multiple dwelling purpose-built	·89	— ·35
2 Outside wc	·90	— ·54
14 Council renting		— ·88
7 Professional and managerial group		·53
6 Unskilled group		— ·52
32 Lacking hot water		— ·43
30 Travel to work		— ·37
23 Sex ratio		— ·32
25 Mobility within area		— ·31
5 Manufacturing workers		— ·31
27 Distribution workers		·31

Variables 14, Council renting and 19, Private renting have been eliminated from the multiple correlation matrix because of multicollinearity.

IV Housing Tenure Variable 14

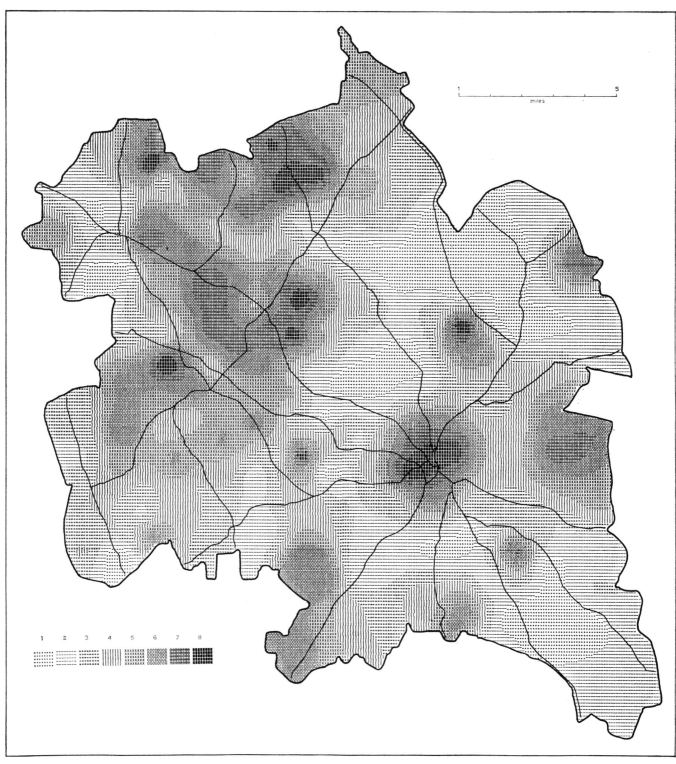

Source: 1966 Census Ward Data, Base Map prepared by The Centre for Urban and Regional Studies, University of Birmingham

14 Conurbation The percentage of dwellings that are rented from local authorities

Maximum included in highest level only

1	**2**	**3**	**4**	**5**	**6**	**7**	**8**
0·00–11·00	11·00–22·00	22·00–33·00	33·00–44·00	44·00–55·00	55·00–66·00	66·00–77·00	77·00–88·00

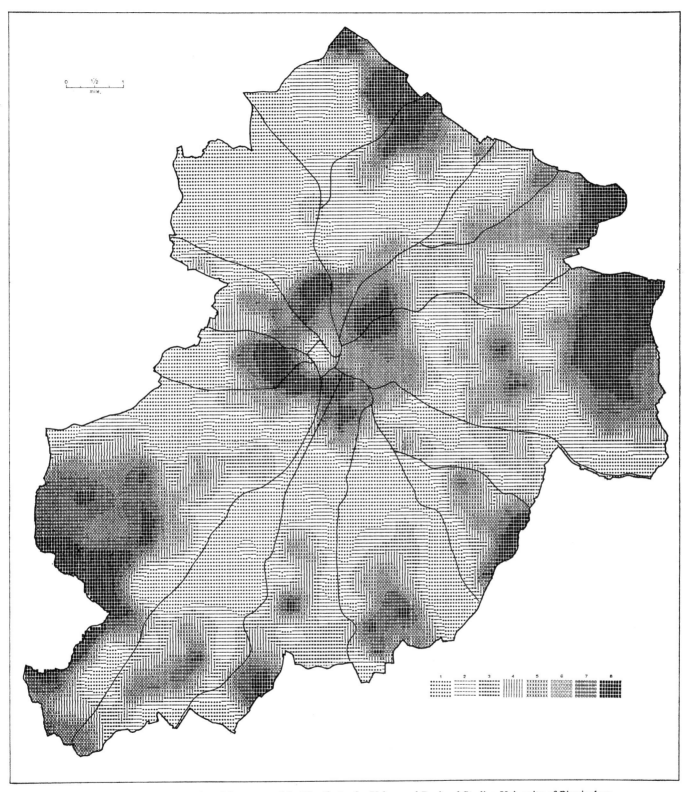

Source: 1966 Enumeration-District Data, Base Map prepared by The Centre for Urban and Regional Studies, University of Birmingham

14 Birmingham The percentage of dwellings that are rented from local authorities

Maximum included in highest level only

1	2	3	4	5	6	7	8
0·00–12·50	12·50–25·00	25·00–37·50	37·50–50·00	50·00–62·50	62·50–75·00	75·00–87·50	87·50–100·00

The percentage of dwellings rented from local authorities

Dwellings rented from local authorities form a distinctive and important sector of the British housing stock. They have been built since the First War with the aid of central government subsidies to provide adequate accommodation at low rents for poor families. Most councils built large estates between the wars, especially during the late 1920s and 1930s. Since 1950, the building of council estates has continued at an increasing pace, in many areas exceeding the numbers of privately built houses. In some cases, these houses have been sold to private individuals, especially in the older estates, but not in sufficient numbers to change the general character of the areas. Some of the socio–economic distinctions between areas of privately and publicly owned housing have become blurred by the general affluence of the postwar period. As we shall see, however, there are still considerable differences of emphasis between them in the West Midlands, at least at the level of generalization with which we are concerned in using the census data.

A complicating factor in recent decades has been the effect of local authority urban renewal schemes in the large cities and conurbations. These commonly have three phases of progress: the purchase (sometimes compulsorily) of privately owned property in areas scheduled for demolition; the removal of most of the residential and commercial buildings from these areas and, finally, the rebuilding of dwellings with their associated services to modern standards. Where the redevelopment is comprehensive, only about one half of the original population numbers can be rehoused in the same areas. Urban renewal has added an important new element to the British urban scene, increasing the areas owned by local authorities, near the centres of cities rather than in the traditional suburban council estates. The time needed to complete the three stages of redevelopment means that where large-scale schemes are in progress, as in Birmingham and some of the Black Country boroughs, 'council renting' may include a number of sub-standard slum dwellings awaiting demolition for several years. These are often 'rehabilitated' at some expense to provide

minimum standards of amenity during the waiting period but their quality nevertheless remains poor. Also, in considering redevelopment, quite large parts of the inner areas of cities remain unoccupied during the demolition and rebuilding phases. Each of these stages needs to be taken into account in interpreting the maps of council housing. In the West Midlands Conurbation large redevelopment schemes were still under way in 1966, especially in Birmingham. In that year, 26·7 per cent of dwellings in England and Wales were rented from local councils. Urban industrial areas, however, generally have a high proportion of council dwellings in response to the needs of their working-class industrial populations. The West Midlands Conurbation had 39·9 per cent of council houses and the city of Birmingham, 40·5 per cent.

The local representation of council housing, like that of owner-occupied housing, has a wide range of values in the Conurbation. The ward values vary from 0 to 88 per cent, while again the Birmingham enumeration districts have the full 0–100 per cent range. Concentrations of council-owned dwellings are much more scattered through the built-up area of the Conurbation than are areas of predominantly privately owned houses. In Birmingham, however, the inner areas and the outer zones of the city, following its boundaries, provide distinct patterns (with more than 66 per cent). In the Black Country the central areas, in a crescent around Wednesbury, large areas of eastern and north-eastern Wolverhampton, and a zone on the north between Wednesfield and Bloxwich are each important. Other areas of local concentration occur to the east of central Dudley and in Smethwick. There is a single concentration in north-eastern Sutton Coldfield but generally, of course, Sutton Coldfield and Solihull, as well as the Streetly–Great Barr–Handsworth Wood area and the western and southern fringes of the Black Country have less than 22 per cent of council housing.

The pattern in the Black Country reflects its long-established subdivided pattern of local authority areas (see frontispiece). Until the boundary revisions of 1965, the Black Country half of the Conurbation was administered by 22 authorities. This meant that each local authority normally had to satisfy its

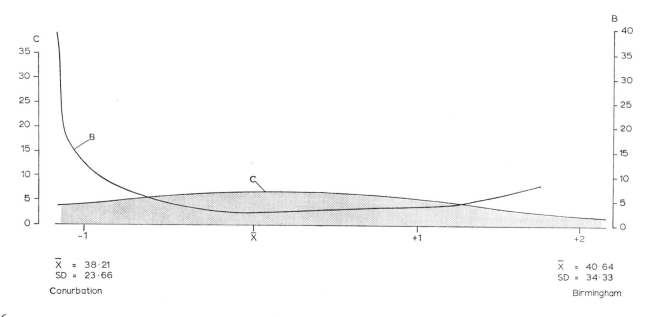

X̄ = 38·21
SD = 23·66

Conurbation

X̄ = 40·64
SD = 34·33

Birmingham

council housing needs within very restricted boundaries, on land scattered through the built-up area, either taken from open space, reclaimed from dereliction or created by the demolition of old housing areas. Unlike Birmingham, they were not able to acquire large new areas on the periphery of the built-up area in advance of its expansion, with the exception of some local authorities on the northern boundary, at Wolverhampton, Wednesfield, Willenhall and Walsall.

The typical result of the evolution of public housing in large cities is indicated in Birmingham. The areas of original council house building are suburban, in interwar and postwar estates, alongside the equivalent growth of privately built housing areas. According to the 1966 Census, 125,000 of the dwellings in the city were owner-occupied and 127,710 owned by the local authority. Another 53,000 dwellings were privately rented (48,000 unfurnished). In recent years, however, the emphasis in the city has been very much upon council house building. The City of Birmingham Abstract of Statistics (Reference 4) for 1967 shows that, for example, in 1966, 4,702 houses, flats and maisonettes were completed by the corporation (1,924 in 1961), and only 1,532 (989) by private builders. Many of these council houses (1,925) were built in the Erdington ward where the Castle Bromwich airfield site was being developed in the mid-1960s. The other areas of active building were nearly all in the south-west of the city, in Kings Norton (752 council houses completed in the ward), Brandwood ward – around Kings Heath – (404) and Weoley (278). The private housing effort was also concentrated into these south-western areas where most of the remaining open land in the city was located. 2,500 of the corporation dwellings were in buildings of 3 or more storeys height but in 1966 tall buildings were becoming less important compared with previous years (variable 15).

The importance of redevelopment in the programme of council house building (Reference 28) can be judged by the fact that, of 7,900 families rehoused by the local authority within the city in 1966, only 2,900 came from the waiting list which contained 38,000 families at the beginning of the year. About 3,900 families were rehoused because of demolition for slum clearance and other reconstruction needs such as road

building. The remaining families (about 1,100) were rehoused for various other special reasons. Between 1947 and 1966, 47,428 houses were acquired for slum clearance and, since 29,244 had been demolished between 1945 and 1966, probably up to 15,000 occupied slum houses were owned by the corporation at the end of 1966. In that year the reconditioning of 10,600 houses in clearance areas was completed or in progress and over 4,000 were demolished.

Thus the major council housing areas in Birmingham are still in the outer parts of the city: in Kingstanding, on the north of the city; the Castle Bromwich airfield site (to the north-east); in Shard End, Stechford and Kitts Green (east); Hall Green (south-east); Billesley, Kings Norton and Northfield (south); and Bartley Green, Weoley Castle and Rednal (south-west). Nevertheless, the central areas occupy a prominent place in current housing policy, if only because redevelopment displaces half of the former numbers of residents who have to be rehoused. The five redevelopment areas, Newtown and Nechells Green on the north of the city centre, and Ladywood, Lee Bank and Highgate to the south, stand out clearly on the map of the city (see page 103). Also, council-owned housing now includes many of the dwellings on land between these areas, outside the recent zone of rebuilding. These areas will be the subject of the next phase of reconstruction in the city, to commence in the early 1970s (Reference 28).

The correlation analysis confirms that, in contrast to areas mainly of owner-occupied houses in the Conurbation, wards with high proportions of council housing are also characterized by high proportions of manufacturing and unskilled workers (variables 5 and 6). Dwellings are generally small (variable 16), with high rates of occupation (variable 42 – this is the strongest 'independent' correlation) and low rates of migration from outside the local authority area (variable 17). It has already been remarked that such wards also have high proportions of dwellings with more than two families (variable 8). The enumeration-district analysis of Birmingham provides a more limited range of significant correlations, essentially the same as for the Conurbation wards, with the addition of a strong negative association with areas having high proportions of privately rented dwellings.

Conurbation	Stepwise multiple	Simple
Variable	correlation	correlation
42 Persons per room	·79	·79
24 Fertility ratio	·86	(not significant)
36 2-person households	·90	·36
22 New Commonwealth immigrants	·93	(not significant)
13 Owner-occupied		−·90
16 Dwelling size		−·77
17 Migration into local authority		−·69
7 Professional and managerial group		−·63
8 Households with 2+ families		·59
27 Distribution workers		−·58
6 Unskilled group		·57
5 Manufacturing workers		·56
1 All basic amenities		·41

Birmingham	Stepwise multiple	Simple
Variable	correlation	correlation
16 Dwelling size	·65	−·65
42 Persons per room	·74	·53
17 Migration into local authority	·78	−·53
18 Owner-occupied		−·88
20 Private renting		−·58
30 Professional and managerial group		−·44
2 Outside wc		·40
15 Multiple dwellings purpose-built		·39
25 Mobility within area		·33
22 New Commonwealth immigrants		−·31
6 Unskilled group		−·31
5 Manufacturing workers		·30
27 Distribution workers		−·30

Variables 19, Private renting and 13, Owner-occupied, have been eliminated from the multiple correlation matrix because of multicollinearity.

Source: 1966 Census Ward Data, Base Map prepared by The Centre for Urban and Regional Studies, University of Birmingham

15 Conurbation The percentage of dwellings that were purpose-built as multiple dwellings

Maximum included in highest level only

1	2	3	4	5	6	7	8
0·00–4·00	4·00–8·00	8·00–12·00	12·00–16·00	16·00–20·00	20·00–24·00	24·00–28·00	28·00–32·00

Source: 1966 Enumeration-District Data, Base Map prepared by The Centre for Urban and Regional Studies, University of Birmingham

15 Birmingham The percentage of dwellings that were purpose-built as multiple dwellings

Maximum included in highest level only

1	2	3	4	5	6	7	8
0·00–9·00	9·00–18·00	18·00–27·00	27·00–36·00	36·00–45·00	45·00–54·00	54·00–63·00	63·00–72·00

Variable 15

The percentage of dwellings purpose-built as multiple dwellings

Reference will be made in the next section (variable 19) to 'multiple dwellings' (i.e. more than one dwelling in a single building) that are the result of conversions from originally single dwellings. These are common in certain parts of the Conurbation. In recent years, however, general shortage of land, nationally as well as at the regional and local level in the West Midlands Conurbation, has encouraged a policy of purpose-building relatively high density blocks of flats and maisonettes. Such forms of building existed before the last war, of course, and are traditionally more common in the cities of Scotland and on the continent. The clearing of slums and the rehousing of their inhabitants within confined local authority areas has also generally encouraged a good deal of 'high-rise' building and involved a limited though significant change in English living habits. Considerable controversy surrounds this type of accommodation, both over the social implications of housing for families in blocks of flats and over the relative economies of building such blocks compared with more conventional two-storeyed houses. Not all of the multiple dwellings traced in these maps are necessarily high-rise, however, although a large proportion of them are so. In view of this background, a close association between council house building and purpose-built multiple dwellings might be expected. Private developers have constructed multiple dwellings on a more modest scale, not generally for family living but to suit the needs of certain groups of single people and married couples in the higher income groups.

In the Conurbation in 1966, the Census enumerated 60,000 dwellings in this category, 8·2 per cent of the total number. The proportion in Birmingham was higher, at 9·6 per cent, and both of these proportions were higher than the England and Wales average of 8·1 per cent. The range of values in the Conurbation wards was quite considerable, however, from 0 to 32 per cent, the frequency distribution being strongly positively skewed towards the low values. In Birmingham, the highest value for an enumeration district was 72 per cent of all dwellings.

The Conurbation map shows the importance of the redevelopment areas around central Birmingham in contributing towards the total number of purpose-built multiple dwellings in the Conurbation. They are accompanied by several areas on the periphery of the city. It is a quite common feature of the outskirts of Birmingham to find high-density dwellings, including blocks of flats, overlooking open Green Belt countryside. All of these, of course, are in council housing areas. The Black Country contains about 30,000 of these multiple dwellings but they are generally more scattered throughout the built-up area for reasons that were discussed in considering council house distribution (variable 14). In the Black Country, the building of tall blocks was delayed because of land subsidence problems and areas with more solid foundations have only relatively recently been developed in this way; in Smethwick, Oldbury, parts of the northern areas of West Bromwich and, in lower proportions per ward, at Dudley, Bilston, Willenhall and Wolverhampton.

The detailed map of Birmingham picks out the location of multiple dwellings of this type very precisely. The five redevelopment areas generally exceed 63 per cent representation and the concentration in outer parts of the city includes the council housing areas built during the last decade at Bartley Green, Rubery and Longbridge on the south-west, at Kings Norton on the south and on the north-east where the large housing scheme on the former Castle Bromwich airfield was built in the mid-1960s. Other blocks of recently built council house infilling are noticeable in Harborne and Quinton in the south-western part of the city. Nearer the city centre enumeration districts in Edgbaston have a proportion of more than 36 per cent in purpose-built multiple dwellings and these are almost entirely privately built as part of the Calthorpe Estate redevelopment (see variable 7). They have a different character from the council housing areas.

The correlations for the areas with high proportions of purpose-built multiple dwellings are not very strong for the Conurbation. The principal one is with the proportion of the resident population that has moved from elsewhere in the same local authority during the previous five years (variable 25).

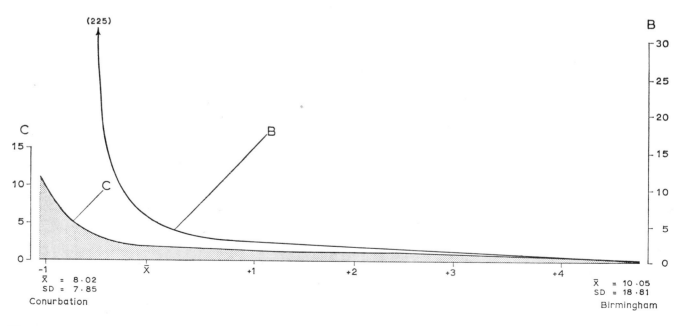

(225)

B

C   B

15

C

10

5

0

    -1   x̄   +1   +2   +3   +4

x̄ = 8·02
SD = 7·85

Conurbation

x̄ = 10·05
SD = 18·81

Birmingham

Relocation of people to these council house areas is the main mechanism by which these flats have been filled. In Birmingham the main association is with the possession of all basic amenities (variable 1), emphasizing the improvement in basic living conditions that these multiple dwellings represent. Apart from movement within the local authority, the other main correlation is with small dwelling size, in terms of numbers of rooms

(variable 16) and council renting. These two, as we saw in discussing the last variable, are closely associated. Council renting, purpose-built multiple dwellings, small dwelling size and recent movement within the local authority form a group of variables in this section that are strongly characteristic of certain areas in the Conurbation.

Conurbation

Variable	Stepwise multiple correlation	Simple correlation
25 Mobility within area	·54	·53
4 Married women working	·60	·38
1 All basic amenities	·62	·24
16 Dwelling size		−·37
42 Persons per room		·36
13 Owner-occupied		−·36
14 Council renting		·34

Birmingham

Variable	Stepwise multiple correlation	Simple correlation
1 All basic amenities	·57	·57
25 Mobility within area	·71	·52
16 Dwelling size		−·40
14 Council renting		·39
4 Married women working		·36
13 Owner-occupied		−·35

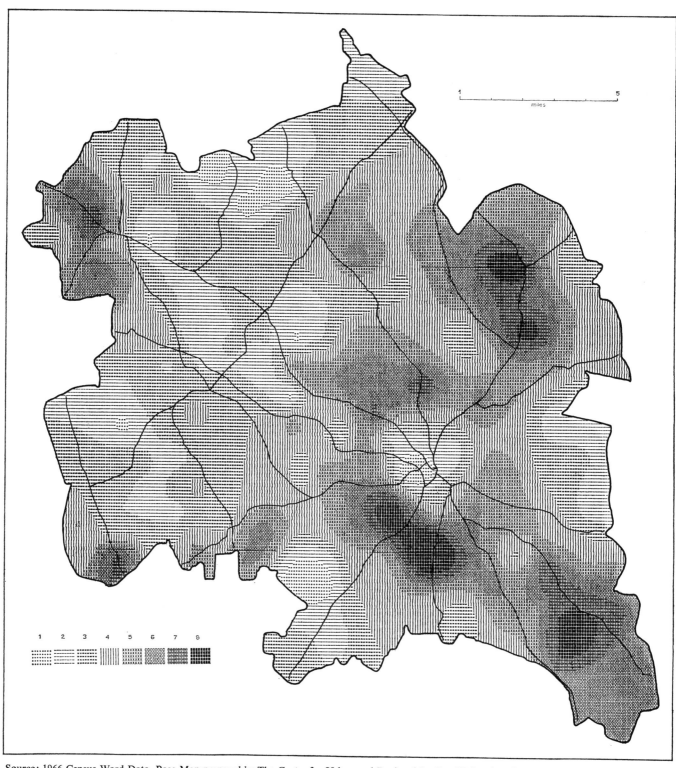

Source: 1966 Census Ward Data, Base Map prepared by The Centre for Urban and Regional Studies, University of Birmingham

16 Conurbation Average dwelling size: number of rooms

Maximum included in highest level only

1	2	3	4	5	6	7	8
4·75–5·00	5·00–5·25	5·25–5·50	5·50–5·75	5·75–6·00	6·00–6·25	6·25–6·50	6·50–6·75

Source: 1966 Enumeration-District Data, Base Map prepared by The Centre for Urban and Regional Studies, University of Birmingham

16 Birmingham Average dwelling size: number of rooms

Maximum included in highest level only

1	2	3	4	5	6	7	8
4·00–4·50	4·50–5·00	5·00–5·50	5·50–6·00	6·00–6·50	6·50–7·00	7·00–7·50	7·50–8·00

Variable 16

Average dwelling size: numbers of rooms

The most direct and simplest measure of a dwelling is its size. Here this is traced in terms of the numbers of rooms, excluding bathrooms, toilets, landings, lobbies, sculleries and other non-'living' spaces. The count for 1966 included kitchens or other rooms used for cooking. No account is made, of course, of the size of rooms themselves. Dwellings, as defined in the Introduction, consist of structurally separate accommodation units, whether houses, flats, maisonettes or even bed-sitting rooms if they have a self-contained bathroom and cooking facilities.

By this measure, the average size of dwellings in the Conurbation was 5·4 rooms per occupied dwelling in 1966, about the same as the national average of 5·5. There are, however, significant differences in the average size of dwellings between different types of tenure. Owner-occupied houses in the Conurbation, for example, have an average size of 5·9 rooms while council-rented dwellings are generally smaller, at 4·9 rooms. Privately rented accommodation in the Conurbation is of about average size between these: 5·4 rooms per dwelling. These figures are about the same as for the whole of England and Wales and, within the Conurbation, the city of Birmingham shows similar average dwelling sizes.

The range of values for individual wards of the Conurbation is from an average of 4·75 to 6·75 rooms per dwelling. In Birmingham, the enumeration-district range of values, as might be expected, is greater, from 4·0 to 8·0 rooms per dwelling. There are only limited concentrations of large housing in a sea of relatively smaller dwellings. The principal zone of consistently large dwellings in the Conurbation (i.e. larger than median value of the range) is around the centre of Birmingham, in an intermediate belt between smaller dwellings in the central areas and outer suburbs of the city. The largest houses and flats are found especially in the south-western sector of the city, with parts of the north-west and of nearby West Bromwich also having relatively more rooms. In these wards, the average size is above 6·00 rooms. The general zone of high values around Birmingham corresponds to the parts of the city built during the latter half of the last century to suit the needs of families that were generally larger than is common today. For this reason it also corresponds to the current zone of 'transitional' social and demographic characteristics that is

traced in detail in the next section. As we shall see, the distribution of the next variable (17), also corresponds to this area in Birmingham. The size and character of the dwellings in this zone are of crucial significance in understanding the attraction that they hold, when subdivided, for single persons, students, immigrants from outside the city and other types of household that do not need or cannot afford to buy standard family houses and do not qualify for council houses.

The physical character of this belt of large dwellings can be explained in terms of the demand for speculative middle-class housing that existed in the late nineteenth century. Today, this type of demand falls upon other places, such as the satellite towns of Sutton Coldfield and Solihull, which emerge clearly on the Conurbation map. These are not areas that have yet outlived their original purpose; they are where the well-to-do middle classes are found today. Again they appear on the Conurbation map for the next variable but are not generally found on the maps in the next section. Sutton Coldfield and Solihull also appear, with the parts of Wolverhampton and southern Stourbridge that stand out on the Conurbation map of this variable, on the maps of relatively high living standard indices, such as car ownership (variable 3). Thus the measure of dwelling size, like that of recent immigration to be shown next, has a double personality: in the Conurbation as a whole it reveals wealthy areas of owner-occupied housing, but in Birmingham taken alone it pinpoints a zone of obsolescence which is very much more complex in character.

Most of the Conurbation, of course, contains small dwellings, both privately owned and rented from local councils. The areas of smallest average size are generally council-owned, however, and this association is particularly strong in Birmingham.

The detailed map of Birmingham throws some light onto the character of the principal zone of large dwellings within the Conurbation. As we shall see, its present occupants exhibit a great variety of socio–economic characteristics. The Edgbaston–Moseley belt in the south-west of the city is most distinctive, although certainly not typical of the whole zone, with average sizes of dwellings consistently above 6·50 rooms and regularly reaching over 7·50.

This is the suburb that grew throughout the nineteenth century and in the first thirty years of the twentieth as the preferred area for the richer entrepreneurial and professional

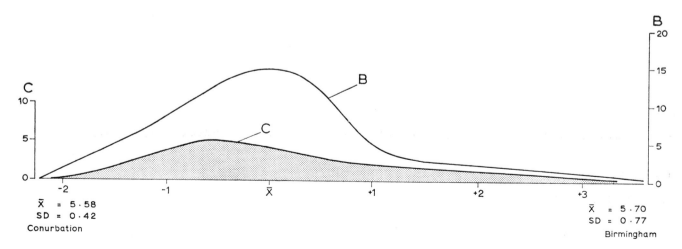

X̄ = 5·58
SD = 0·42
Conurbation

X̄ = 5·70
SD = 0·77
Birmingham

94

classes. Its character has been diluted in recent decades, although the efforts of the major leaseholder, the Calthorpe Estate company, to preserve its character by high-class redevelopment have been moderately successful (see discussion of variable 7). Many of the old houses in the zone have been demolished and rebuilt at a higher (although by modern standards still low) density, while many others have been converted into generally high-cost flats. Outside the Calthorpe Estate properties in Edgbaston, Moseley and Handsworth are becoming subject to the trends found in other parts of this intermediate zone. The map confirms, in fact, that the highly distinctive suburb of Edgbaston is simply a part of the general ring of nineteenth-century housing, built for the relatively spacious demands of the artisan classes of that time. It represents an extreme case and, without the control that has been exercised in recent years by the leaseholder, its character would undoubtedly have radically changed. Section V will demonstrate the complexities of the current situation in other parts of this zone.

The correlation analysis reveals a number of interesting associations with dwelling size. In the Conurbation the strongest is with owner-occupied housing (variable 13), as has already been suggested. Next, there is a strong correlation with areas of professional and distributive workers (variables 7 and 27) as opposed to manufacturing workers. Then, not unexpectedly, there are large numbers of houses converted to flats in these areas of large dwellings (variable 19), and also relatively large proportions of people who have recently moved into the area from outside the local authority (variable 17). These would include both those migrating outwards to the satellite towns of the Conurbation and those moving into the areas of old large houses in Birmingham from outside. In Birmingham, a negative association with areas of council-rented housing is again strong and also the proportion of shared dwellings (variable 18) appears with a relatively high correlation. Other shared facilities (variables 31 and 33) are also significantly correlated with dwelling size in Birmingham and these variables indicate the generally subdivided character of the larger dwellings in the city, unlike those in the prosperous areas of Sutton Coldfield and Solihull.

In general, large dwellings have been built at various times for the middle classes. The older areas have been subject to marked socio–economic changes in recent decades but the newer areas on the periphery of the Conurbation are the places where the prosperous live today.

Conurbation

Variable	Stepwise multiple correlation	Simple correlation
14 Council renting	·77	— ·77
18 Households sharing dwellings	·84	·47
7 Professional and managerial group	·90	·66
15 Multiple dwelling purpose-built	·92	— ·37
38 Unoccupied dwellings	·93	·31
42 Persons per room	·94	— ·67
27 Distribution workers		·68
13 Owner-occupied		·68
5 Manufacturing workers		— ·65
19 Multiple dwellings converted		·60
17 Migration into local authority		·57
37 Skilled workers		— ·56
6 Unskilled group		— ·46
4 Married women working		— ·46
33 Sharing wc		·43
8 Households with 2+ families		— ·42
1 All basic amenities		— ·41

Birmingham

Variable	Stepwise multiple correlation	Simple correlation
14 Council renting	·65	— ·65
18 Households sharing dwellings	·79	·62
38 Unoccupied dwellings	·86	·35
42 Persons per room	·89	— ·30
13 Owner-occupied	·91	·56
25 Mobility into area		·60
33 Sharing wc		·56
31 Sharing hot water		·48
22 New Commonwealth immigrants		·44
19 Multiple dwellings converted		·43
20 Private renting		·41
7 Professional and managerial group		·40

Source: 1966 Census Ward Data, Base Map prepared by The Centre for Urban and Regional Studies, University of Birmingham

17 Conurbation The percentage of the total population that moved into the local authority area during five years before April 1966

Maximum included in highest level only

1	2	3	4	5	6	7	8
0·00–3·50	3·50–7·00	7·00–10·50	10·50–14·00	14·00–17·50	17·50–21·00	21·00–24·50	24·50–28·00

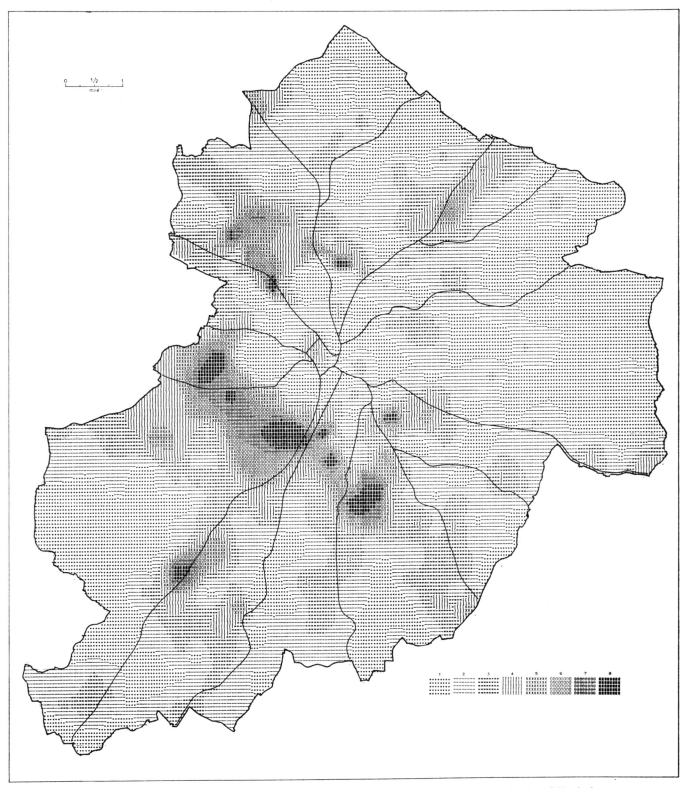

Source: 1966 Enumeration-District Data, Base Map prepared by The Centre for Urban and Regional Studies, University of Birmingham

17 Birmingham The percentage of the total population that moved into the local authority area during five years before April 1966

Maximum included in highest level only

1	2	3	4	5	6	7	8
0·00–3·50	3·50–7·00	7·00–10·50	10·50–14·00	14·00–17·50	17·50–21·00	21·00–24·50	24·50–28·00

Variable 17

The percentage of the total population that moved into the local authority area during the five years before April 1966

The 1966 Sample Census, which took place in April of that year, obtained a good deal of information on migration into and within Britain during the previous five years (see also variables 21 and 22). The index shown here provides a simple measure of areas that had the most changed populations in 1966 compared with 1961. It is obviously affected by the variable sizes of local authority areas: for example, a movement of residence over a distance of four miles within Birmingham would not be recorded by this measure, although in the Black Country it would probably imply a change of local authority area. Thus on the Conurbation map the degree of movement of local residents in the Birmingham half of the built-up area is relatively under-represented and the city emerges as a low area. The detailed map of Birmingham, therefore, has a special significance for this variable.

Another aspect of these maps that deserves emphasis is the variety of types of moves that must underlie the patterns. Migration into new accommodation within the West Midlands Conurbation falls into at least three types: a) movement of local people into new houses in nearby local authority areas in the Conurbation; b) the movement of people into the Conurbation from elsewhere in Britain; c) the movement of people from overseas to take up their first British residence in the Conurbation. Each of these types has a particular interest in the context of the current problems of the West Midlands but it is very difficult to disentangle them using the maps alone.

The published statistics of migration for the Sample Census are contained in a special volume for the West Midlands (Reference 11). Many details are displayed there that cannot be reproduced here. In summary, however, migration from one address to another within the Conurbation affected 593,000 people during the 1961–6 period, about 25 per cent of the total population. In Birmingham, 24 per cent of the population had moved within its area during this period and the figures for the other authorities in the Conurbation ranged from 12–13 per cent in Solihull, Sutton Coldfield and Aldridge–Brownhills to over 19 per cent in the large central boroughs of the Black Country: Dudley, Wolverhampton, Walsall and West Bromwich. These figures, of course, may be affected by the sizes, shapes and locations of the local authority areas, but internal

migration would be expected to reach higher levels in the established built-up areas than in the newly developed areas of the Conurbation. In fact, the geographical extent of the main Conurbation boroughs outside Birmingham, except for the smaller boroughs of Stourbridge and Halesowen, do not differ greatly (see frontispiece).

Movements into the areas from outside are of more direct interest here. In the five-year period under study, 127,000 people, equivalent to 5·3 per cent of the population, moved into the Conurbation from outside. In Birmingham, the proportion was 7·1 per cent of the resident population in 1966. The figures for the rest of the Conurbation ranged from over 20 per cent in Aldridge–Brownhills, Solihull and Sutton Coldfield to less than 9 per cent in Walsall, Wolverhampton and Warley. In spite of the problem of non-uniform local authority areas, these figures provide an indication of the average 'newness' of the populations within these well-defined districts of the Conurbation. In the next section we shall deal in some detail with migration from overseas but, for comparative purposes, the contribution of areas outside Great Britain between 1961 and 1966 (including Ireland as well as other overseas sources) was 2 per cent of the resident population for the Conurbation as a whole. 2·7 per cent for Birmingham, and ranged in the other local authorities, from 2·4 per cent in Wolverhampton, through 1·8 per cent in Walsall and Warley, 1·4 per cent in West Bromwich, 1·3 per cent in Sutton Coldfield and generally less than 1 per cent elsewhere. The balance of migration during this period confirms the trends referred to in the Introduction to the atlas. There is a net loss of population by migration in the central boroughs of the Conurbation, including Birmingham (amounting to 5·4 per cent of the resident population over the five-year period), Walsall (1·4 per cent), West Bromwich 0·2 per cent), Wolverhampton (1·4 per cent) and Warley (1·3 per cent). On the other hand, large gains were made in Aldridge–Brownhills (10·3 per cent), Stourbridge (4·2 per cent), Sutton Coldfield (3·8 per cent), Solihull (3·5 per cent) and also Dudley (3·4 per cent) which contains the areas around Kingswinford and Sedgley on the west of the Conurbation where much new housing has recently taken place. The gains in Sutton Coldfield and Solihull were less than might be expected from the high rates of gross immigration mentioned earlier, because these also exhibit the highest percentage rates of gross emigration (around 17–18 per cent) to other areas.

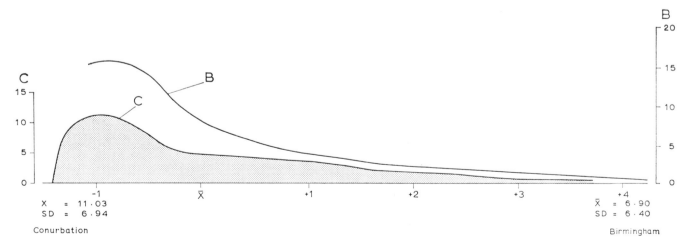

98

The general 'turnover' of houses in these prosperous areas is significantly higher than elsewhere in the Conurbation. Aldridge–Brownhills M.B. had the largest net gain through migration because it has catered less for the mobile professional and managerial groups (see variable 7) and more for the residentially more stable skilled manual and white collar workers.

The ward map of the Conurbation confirms the overwhelming importance of movement to its peripheral local authorities. The range of values shown here spreads from 0 to 28 per cent of the local residents that had moved into the respective local authority areas during the previous five years. In Birmingham, the enumeration-district percentages also range from 0 to 28 per cent. In large parts of Aldridge, Streetly, much of Sutton Coldfield and Great Barr on the north-east of the Conurbation, more than 21 per cent of the ward populations had moved in during the 1961–6 period. Similarly, Solihull, on the south-east, Stourbridge on the south-west and areas around Kingswinford on the west stand out clearly.

Within the city of Birmingham, areas that appear as only pale shadows on the Conurbation map are shown in sharper relief on the enumeration-district map. The main feature is the Edgbaston–Moseley zone to the south-west of the city, which has already been referred to as possessing the main concentrations of professional and managerial groups (variable 7), large houses (variable 16), and, more significantly as we shall see, houses subdivided into flats (variable 19). Enumeration districts with more than 21 per cent of their residents who have recently moved in are common. The level elsewhere in the city (which can be directly compared, since we are here dealing with only one local authority area) is generally less than 7 per cent. Other areas of recently arrived residents form rather isolated nodes in the north-west, in Handsworth, and the south-east, in Sparkbrook. Certain of the concentrations in Edgbaston and further south-west between Selly Oak and Northfield are probably caused by student hostels and a good deal of the rest of the pattern may also be attributed to this particular class of itinerant flat dweller in this part of the city. Another group of immigrant to the city, of course, has come from overseas (including Ireland), but the general pattern of location here does not very closely resemble

that of immigrants traced in the next section under variables 21 and 22. It is clear that the contribution of overseas immigrants to the general level of movement within and into the Conurbation and city was not in any way overwhelming during the 1961–6 period. In fact they contributed 22,000 of the total number of 75,000 persons living in Birmingham in 1966 who were not there in 1961.

It is obvious from a comparison of the maps that the character of the movement shown on the Conurbation map differs considerably from that shown in detail on the Birmingham map, in the same way as with variable 16. The correlation analysis pinpoints this difference very effectively. The analysis of the Conurbation ward data shows that areas with high proportions of recent immigrants at this large scale of study also have higher than average proportions of owner-occupied houses (variable 13), professional and managerial workers (variable 7), workers in the distributive trades (variable 27), large dwellings (variable 16) and high car ownership rates (variable 3). They are not areas with high proportions of council houses (variable 14), of unskilled workers (variable 6), or women working (variable 34), of two-family households (variable 8), of overcrowding (variable 42) or of manufacturing workers (variable 5). In Birmingham, however a very different type of distinction is found between areas of recent immigration and the more stable suburbs. Most of the correlations are positive and show that immigrants to the city live in areas where there are larger than average dwellings (variable 16) but where these also tend to be shared (variable 18), along with the basic amenities such as w.c.s, hot water and a sink and stove (variables 33, 31 and 35). Tenancy is more often under private landlords (variable 20) than elsewhere in the city and there are, as would be expected, more New Commonwealth immigrants (variable 22) than average. The main significant negative correlation is with council housing (variable 14), which, almost by definition, cannot be occupied by new arrivals in the city.

This association of characteristics places the Birmingham pattern of recent immigrants in a different factor from that of the Conurbation. More about the types of area where they live will now be examined in Section V.

Conurbation

Variable	Stepwise multiple correlation	Simple correlation
13 Owner-occupied	·75	·75
10 Age 45–65	·82	−·29
37 Skilled group	·85	−·37
25 Mobility within area	·87	−·49
7 Professional and managerial group		·72
14 Council renting		−·69
6 Unskilled group		−·62
34 Female employment		−·59
16 Dwelling size		·57
3 Cars per household		·56
8 Households with 2+ families		−·53
27 Distribution workers		·52
42 Persons per room		−·52
5 Manufacturing workers		−·50
36 2-person households		−·50
30 Travel to work		−·49
25 Mobility within area		−·49
2 Outside wc		−·41

Birmingham

Variable	Stepwise multiple correlation	Simple correlation
18 Households sharing dwellings	·73	·73
14 Council renting	·80	−·52
27 Distribution workers	·82	·26
22 New Commonwealth immigrants	·85	·60
7 Professional and managerial group	·86	·40
13 Owner-occupied	·87	·35
33 Sharing w c		·70
16 Dwelling size		·60
31 Sharing hot water		·59
20 Private renting		·57
35 Sharing sink and stove		·51
19 Multiple dwelling converted		·50
37 Skilled group		−·41
29 Households without families		·41

V Introduction

The variables in this section group into factor 2 in the enumeration-district analysis for Birmingham. They therefore trace the most important geographical distinction in the city, after that based upon occupations and employment discussed in Section II. Characteristics are here being measured which display their variation most clearly at the small scale of analysis allowed by the enumeration-district data. In the Conurbation ward analysis the factor is only the fourth and the wards appear to be too crude a form of spatial measurement to identify the essentially local distinctions with which we are here concerned.

The factor brings together the following variables, in the order of their 'contribution': the percentage of households sharing dwellings, sharing a w.c. and sharing hot water (these three are strongly related in their occurrence); households living at more than 1½ persons per room (an index of overcrowding); households sharing a sink and stove (another sharing index, but less consistently related to the factor than the others); the proportion of the population born in 'New Commonwealth' countries (defined by the General Register Office to include those from the Commonwealth and Colonies, excluding Australia, New Zealand and Canada); the proportion of dwellings that are 'multiple' (e.g. in flats and maisonettes), converted from single houses; the proportion of the population born in Northern Ireland and Eire; and, finally, the rate of unemployment. Also contributing to this factor in Birmingham is the proportion of dwellings that are rented from private landlords but in the Conurbation as a whole this is more closely related to the variables of Section I. It has already been pointed out that, in Birmingham, variables 16 and 17 have high values in similar areas to some of the variables in this section, although for the Conurbation at large they contribute more to the factor of Section IV.

The variables, when combined, describe areas with high proportions of shared dwellings and basic amenities, privately rented accommodation, immigrants from all sources outside the respective local authority areas, overcrowding and unemployment. A common physical condition for the accumulation of these features is a stock of large obsolescent houses (variable 16). Generally speaking, however, the maps in this section show no exact correspondence of pattern between the variables; they overlap in their geographical extent and combine in different ways from area to area, producing sectors of varying character.

Several of these variables, particularly 'lodging-house' private renting, shared dwellings and the concentration of immigrants, have been used by urban sociologists and geographers for the past forty years to measure the residential aspects of the 'zone of transition' that appears to be a common feature of the western city. Processes first studied in detail by Park and Burgess (Reference 23) in Chicago have in fact been traced in Birmingham by Rex and Moore, although with substantial modification and refinement of approach (References 24, 25). In the Sparkbrook study, Rex and Moore made a detailed sociological survey of a particular part of the 'zone of transition' (sometimes called the 'twilight zone') in Birmingham. Sparkbrook, to the south-east of the city centre was chosen because it had special problems of community and racial relations. It appears, of course, on our maps and we have nothing to add to the sociological insights that were derived through that fascinating piece of work. The maps demonstrate, however, that in using any 'objective' and static census index of 'transitional' qualities, a zone of much wider extent and variety emerges (see Reference 13 for a broader discussion of 'transitional' qualities).

The theory which attempts to explain the 'zone of transition' embodies general ideas about competition between social groups for the limited supply of various types of housing within a city. Because of its age and size, housing in the zone is not favoured by the stable family groups which live both in established working and middle-class suburbs. Groups in the zone of transition are therefore normally recent arrivals in

Conurbation factor 4			Other high factor loading		
Variable	Factor loading	Commun-ality	Section	Factor	Factor loading
33 Sharing wc*	·950	·930			
18 Households sharing dwellings*	·932	·935			
31 Sharing hot water*	·912	·872			
35 Sharing sink and stove*	·778	·799	I	1	·393
19 Multiple dwellings converted*	·677	·687	II	5	·432
21 Irish immigrants*	·609	·639	I	1	·414
22 New Commonwealth immigrants*	·600	·740	I	1	·539
29 Households without families	·587	·880	I	1	·565
			IV	2	−·324
			III	3	−·324
39 Households occupied 1½+ persons per room*	·572	·827	I	1	·522
			IV	2	−·351
20 Private renting	·459	·713	I	1	·588
41 Unemployment rate*	·417	·535	I	1	·466
			IV	2	−·378
37 Skilled group	−·301	·488	II	5	−·523

Birmingham factor 2			Other high factor loading		
Variable	Factor loading	Commun-ality	Section	Factor	Factor loading
18 Households sharing dwellings*	−·940	·891			
33 Sharing wc	−·934	·881			
31 Sharing hot water*	−·867	·782			
35 Sharing sink and stove*	−·783	·723	II	1	·313
22 New Commonwealth immigrants*	−·698	·711	II	1	·382
19 Multiple dwelling converted*	−·622	·477			
29 Households without families	−·610	·765	I	3	−·463
16 Dwelling size	−·592	·724	IV	4	−·550
39 Households occupied 1½+ persons per room*	−·584	·742	II	1	·387
			I	3	−·333
			III	5	·311
20 Private renting*	−·563	·464			
21 Irish immigrants*	−·528	·451	I	3	−·307
37 Skilled group	·523	·369			
41 Unemployment rate*	−·319	·260	I	3	·466
			IV	2	−·378

* Principal variables in this factor.

Source: 1966 Enumeration-District Data, Base Map prepared by The Centre for Urban and Regional Studies, University of Birmingham

Section V Birmingham factor 2 The Zone of Transition

Factor score, maximum included in highest level only

1	2	3	4	5	6	7	8
−9·00−−7·25	−7·25−−5·50	−5·50−−3·75	−3·75−−2·00	−2·00−−0·25	−0·25−1·50	1·50−3·25	3·25−5·00

the city from outside: single persons and poor families that do not have access to the 'accepted' housing areas, for a variety of reasons. In Birmingham, Rex and Moore elaborated the character of competition for housing in the British context, emphasizing that it was not simply for the use of sites and buildings, but also more generally for all available resources of housing in the city. In Britain, the allocation of only a part of these resources is by market forces, in the private sector where family incomes need to be consistent and above a certain level (variable 13). Elsewhere, as we have seen (variable 14), a large part of the competition is regulated by public policy. The allocation of council tenancies is not arbitrary, of course, but automatically favours long-established residents in the city, living in average family units. Thus immigrant groups from anywhere outside the city or those who do not live in family groups, such as single persons, students or even married couples without children, are funnelled into the zone of transition as effectively, if not more effectively, by public policy as by market forces. In emphasizing this, Rex and Moore hoped to clarify the importance of future public housing policy in preventing the development of racial and socially deprived ghettos in British cities.

The authors of the Sparkbrook study pointed out that the zone of transition, as they studied it in their detailed case example, contains very varied types of accommodation and categories of occupant (Chapter 12). A wider view, as made possible for example by the data of these maps, seems to extend the range of this variety almost to the limits of a coherent definition of a 'zone'. In fact, variety is probably the most remarkable trait of the zone, in contrast to the uniformity of the more stable inner and outer suburbs traced in earlier sections of this atlas. This variety certainly exacerbates the problems of providing consistent planning policies to deal with its ills. There are good reasons for taking each of the variables in this section as an indicator for 'transitional' qualities but when they are combined their overlapping distributions tend to blur any composite definition. Shared dwellings, for example, are more common than elsewhere in the Conurbation but, even in the areas where they are most prevalent, they account for only about one half of the number of households. Privately rented accommodation, the lodging houses and flats that are favoured by urban sociologists to mark 'transition', seldom form more than 40 per cent of the dwellings. We have already seen how immigrants in the 1961–6 period concentrated into certain areas (variable 17) but New Commonwealth and Irish immigrants (variables 22 and 21) are important only in quite small areas and their proportions in individual enumeration districts in Birmingham seldom exceeds 30 per cent and 15 per cent respectively. Although Rex and Moore state 'what is segregated (in the zone of transition) is a problem area. All forms of life which are unacceptable according to welfare state standards are confined there' (page 279), problems are not the uniform result of combining the characteristics described here. 'Transitional' qualities in an area, such as privately rented accommodation, recent immigration from outside the city, large dwellings and even, to some extent, shared dwellings may also be favoured by relatively well-off single persons and married couples. After all, Edgbaston and Moseley, which are prominent on several of the maps in this section, also stand out on the map of professional and managerial socio–economic groupings in Birming-

ham (variable 7). It is undeniable that certain parts of the 'transition zone', objectively defined, are social problem areas of profound seriousness for public housing policy. The processes of transition as reflected by census measures nevertheless seem to produce a wider variety of social area than the authors of the Sparkbrook Survey would suggest.

The factor map for Birmingham, of course, provides a composite image of the distribution of these 'transitional' indices. The light areas are those where this factor scores high and the dark areas, in contrast, are the 'stable' areas, particularly in the mainly council-owned inner zone (see variable 14) and in many outer suburban areas. The main zone of shared amenities, privately rented property, overcrowding and immigration is, in fact, in the Edgbaston–Moseley–Hall Green belt on the south of the city. Certain parts of this belt are undergoing rapid social change but it is not generally one of social deprivation, nor indeed of any particular social cohesion. Other areas that are important for this factor are more isolated and scattered in the city but they contain the more pressing social problems, as catalogued by Rex and Moore: parts of Erdington on the north-east of the city; parts of Small Heath, Acocks Green and Sparkbrook in the south-east; the old parts of Selly Oak on the south-west; and, in a marked area to the north-west of the city centre, in Soho and Handsworth.

Quite large numbers of people in any city need accommodation that might be regarded as substandard for family housing, often as a temporary phase during their lives. This need is fulfilled by private landlords, often in converted old houses. The standards of family housing are not necessarily appropriate for single workers or students, for example, and privately rented flats in large houses may even be relatively prestigious for certain social groups. The key to an understanding of the measures displayed in this section is that they pick out a specialized type of accommodation for a particular minority demand in the city; the antithesis, as it were, of the 'average' family demand. Only when such families are forced to live in these circumstances of shared and rented dwellings because of an inadequate supply of family housing in the city, either at the right price in the private sector or at the right time for council housing, does overcrowding and social distress result. It is unfortunate that in the conditions of recent years this has occurred for a proportion of immigrant families. Nevertheless, even in the case of immigrants, a considerable number of them are single men, and this type of accommodation, if in fair physical condition, is not unsuitable.

The fact remains that a supply of privately rented and relatively inexpensive accommodation, which may involve a degree of shared amenities, is a legitimate response to a certain category of housing need. The undesirable aspects of the areas plotted in this section are more a result of a general shortage of family accommodation than of the nature of the dwellings in themselves.

Essentially, these problems can be solved only at a city or even ultimately at a regional scale, with the provision of an adequate housing stock to cater for future population and social developments. Within the areas of 'transition', however, much needs to be done, in terms of both physical renewal and conservation. The massive post-war schemes of urban renewal (see variable 14), which have transformed most of the old working-class slums of Birmingham and the Black Country, have not of course affected the problem areas within the zones of transition except, in some cases, by the transference there of some of the Conurbation's more intractable social problems. In considering measures for preventing the future decline in character of the zones, the different nature of their problems compared with the older slums may demand policies that are perhaps rather more subtle than wholesale demolition and rebuilding. A combination of holding measures to prevent further deterioration, housing and area rehabilitation schemes to promote improvement, and rebuilding projects to provide new area amenities needs to be worked out. In particular, any feelings of deprivation by the communities living in these areas must be alleviated.

In fact, tentative plans for redeveloping some of those areas were prepared in Birmingham even before the acceleration of social change that they have experienced since the late 1950s. As long ago as 1955, shortly after the first phase of redevelopment in the city started, Future Redevelopment Areas were designated to deal comprehensively with the next worst areas. These contained 30,000 dwellings, about the same number as in the first phase areas, although their more varied nature will necessitate a smaller proportion of demolitions. Some of the Future Redevelopment Areas in Birmingham have already been rebuilt, where blocks of land were readily available, but the main effort of redevelopment will follow the completion of the first post-war generation of redevelopment areas, after 1970. The strategy of rebuilding will concentrate upon the rapid redevelopment of the worst nodes of unfit housing and poor environment.

Parts of the zone of transition shown in our maps will be changed by these schemes, especially in the St Andrews area, to the east of the city centre, South Aston to the north and the Boulton area to the west. Events since the late 1950s, however, have changed the housing situation in wider areas than these, resulting in new overcrowding and physical decay in multi-occupied, often privately rented large houses. 140,000 houses in the city outside the redevelopment areas were built before 1914 and many of these are liable to this type of change. Following the 1968 Town and Country Planning Act, powers are now available for local authorities to promote localized rehabilitation and conservation schemes, without the time-consuming disturbance and high expense of wholesale redevelopment. This Act augmented previous legislation which provided Improvement Grants for the installation of adequate basic amenities in structurally sound dwellings. Local authorities were also already able to prevent the development of 'non-conforming' land uses and the uncontrolled conversion of single dwellings to multi-occupation. The part of the 1968 Act which is particularly applicable to the transitional areas allows local improvement within relatively small 'action areas'. Thus, with the additional measures in the 1969 Housing Act for improving houses and their environments, the hope is that the life of old areas can also be improved by introducing more open space, schools and garages and by controlling traffic flows. Unfit property may be demolished to make way for new facilities and local communities can participate in the implementation and planning of these schemes. In Birmingham, parts of Sparkbrook and the Summerfield area on the west of the city were the first Improvement Areas to be designated under this Act in 1969.

None of these measures will solve the fundamental social problems of the worst sectors of the zone of transition. It is even feared that they may accentuate the 'ghetto' aspects of their social life. The need to assimilate overcrowded families into the total housing stock available to the city obviously remains the fundamental problem. Nevertheless, if the general housing shortage problem can be solved over the next decade (and this depends, as we explained in the Introduction, upon the effective implementation of regional housing strategies), the possibility now exists of reversing the processes of physical decay and social estrangement that have traditionally made the zone of transition an inevitable problem.

Five variables have been selected for display in this section: the proportion of households sharing dwellings, which forms one of the primary indices and is representative of all the measures of shared amenities; the proportion of dwellings that are flats and maisonettes converted from old houses; the proportion of dwellings rented from private landlords – a crucial index of housing tenure associated with the zone of transition; and two measures of immigration – the proportion of residents born in Ireland and in the New Commonwealth.

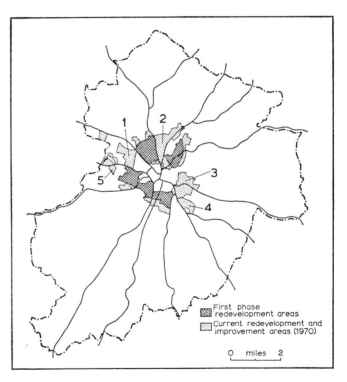

Redevelopment and improvement areas in Birmingham

The 'first phase' Redevelopment Areas have now largely been completed. The current Redevelopment Areas (formerly 'Future Redevelopment Areas') include:

1 Boulton
2 South Aston
3 St Andrews

The first two Improvement Areas were:

4 Sparkbrook
5 Summerfield

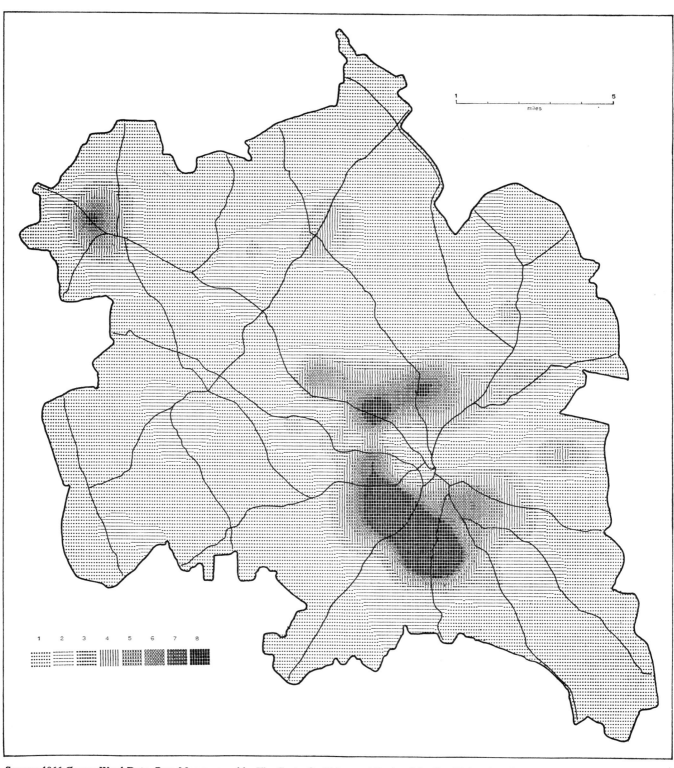

Source: 1966 Census Ward Data, Base Map prepared by The Centre for Urban and Regional Studies, University of Birmingham

18 Conurbation The percentage of households sharing dwellings

Maximum included in highest level only

1	2	3	4	5	6	7	8
0·00–3·00	3·00–6·00	6·00–9·00	9·00–12·00	12·00–15·00	15·00–18·00	18·00–21·00	21·00–24·00

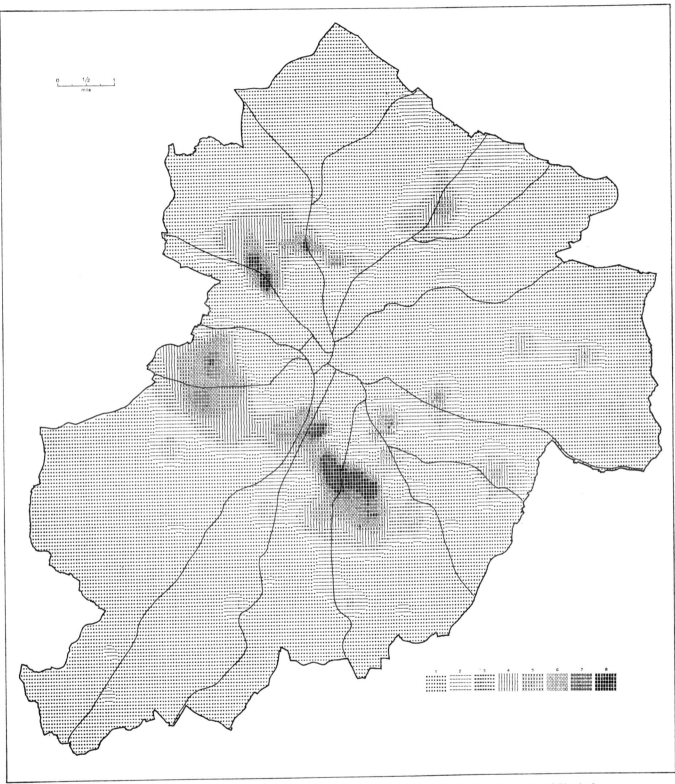

Source: 1966 Enumeration-District Data, Base Map prepared by The Centre for Urban and Regional Studies, University of Birmingham

18 Birmingham The percentage of households sharing dwellings

Maximum included in highest level only

1	2	3	4	5	6	7	8
0·00–8·00	8·00–16·00	16·00–24·00	24·00–32·00	32·00–40·00	40·00–48·00	48·00–56·00	56·00–64·00

Variable 18

The percentage of households sharing dwellings

The sharing of dwellings illustrated in these maps has a particular meaning in the context of the census definitions of the two terms, 'household' and 'dwelling'. These definitions need not be repeated here but should be referred to in the Introduction. This measure has been selected to represent all of the indices of shared amenities used in the census: shared hot water, fixed bath, inside w.c., and sink and stove. The maps of the individual measures show very similar patterns of distribution in both the Conurbation and the city of Birmingham. These patterns contrast, however, with those showing the absence of basic amenities, dealt with in Section I of the atlas. Quite different areas are involved in this section and, as we have suggested, quite different social and housing problems are found there.

In the Conurbation there were over 39,000 households sharing dwellings in 1966 and nearly 29,000 of these were in the city of Birmingham. The distribution of shared dwellings is primarily related to the availability of suitable, relatively large dwellings and a comparison of the patterns of these maps with those of the maps of variable 16 is revealing. Sharing is much more concentrated into Birmingham than the simple availability of large dwellings would suggest. The Conurbation map of this variable emphasizes that it is a particular feature of certain parts of Birmingham, with the second largest urban centre in the Conurbation, Wolverhampton, also having some concentration.

Only 35 per cent of the Conurbation households in shared dwellings enumerated by the census in 1966 had the exclusive use of a hot water tap; only 20 per cent exclusive use of a fixed bath; 25 per cent of an inside w.c.; and about 50 per cent

had to share a sink and stove. In sum, only 16 per cent of households sharing dwellings had sole use of all of these basic amenities. The proportions for England and Wales were generally better than these (for example, 50 per cent of shared dwellings nationally had the exclusive use of a hot water tap, 25 per cent of a fixed bath and 33 per cent of an inside w.c.), so that the quality of shared dwellings in the West Midlands is generally lower than in the country as a whole.

The range of values shown on the map for the Conurbation wards varied from 0 to 24 per cent in 1966. In Birmingham the enumeration-district figures ranged from 0 to 64 per cent Obviously, like the other variables in this section, the sharing of dwellings is highly concentrated into certain areas of the Conurbation and Birmingham. The zones that are so prominent on the Conurbation map, in Birmingham and west of Wolverhampton town centre, had a figure of over 18 per cent. In Birmingham, the enumeration-district values raise the local proportions to over 48 per cent in the most concentrated zones. In this detail, the most dominant area on the Conurbation map emerges as a more broken zone to the south of the city centre, running generally from the northern part of Edgbaston, south-westwards to Moseley. Here large houses, often over forty or fifty years old have been subdivided and occupied particularly by students and other single people. Intermixed with this predominant type are some more permanent migrants from Britain, Ireland and further afield, often single but sometimes in family groups. We have emphasized that the 'transition zone' includes all types of relatively recent arrivals in the city and the typical occupants of this zone of south-west Birmingham are probably young single persons, perhaps sharing accommodation with others, or young married couples. This zone of the city is also notable

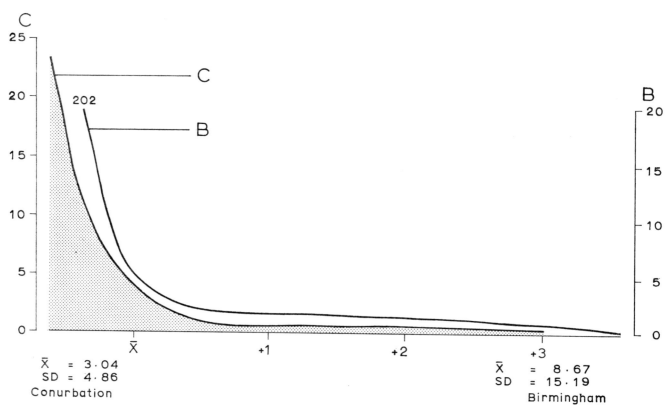

X̄ = 3·04
SD = 4·86
Conurbation

X̄ = 8·67
SD = 15·19
Birmingham

as the main concentration of the professional and managerial groups discussed under variable 7.

In strict terms the quality of this accommodation is poor but, at least in this area of Birmingham, it is often occupied by groups of people who generally do not regard it in any sense as a permanent place to live. In the north-west of the city, however, there is another, less consistent zone of shared dwellings, in the Soho area of Handsworth. Here there seems to be a greater emphasis upon single working men and families in shared accommodation and there are larger proportions of overseas immigrants (Irish and New Commonwealth, variables 21 and 22). This is probably a greater problem area for housing policy, since it is generating a long-term need for family housing in the city.

The highest correlations with this variable are with the other indices of shared amenities that have already been discussed (variable 31, 33 and 35). After these, the most significant correlation is with areas having high proportions of households without families (variable 29) emphasizing the single-person element in areas of shared dwellings. In Birmingham, Irish and New Commonwealth immigrant groups (variables 21 and 22) are strongly associated with areas of shared dwellings although, as we shall see, this association is probably weighted by their high proportions of single men. Another interesting pair of correlations is with areas having larger than average dwelling size (variable 16), as expected from our introductory remarks to this section, and with the overcrowding index (variable 39, proportion of households living at more than $1\frac{1}{2}$ persons per room). Shared dwellings are normally found in areas of converted old houses, so that the association with multiple dwellings converted to that use (variable 19) is also to be expected.

The majority character of these areas of shared dwellings should therefore be fairly clear. They are not necessarily areas of social distress, but of social instability arising from the character of the groups that choose to live in this manner. In some areas, however, problems may arise because others, whose aim is to be more permanently housed, are having to share their living conditions with other households.

Conurbation

Variable	Stepwise multiple correlation	Simple correlation
29 Households without families	·72	·72
16 Dwelling size	·82	·47
42 Persons per room	·88	(not significant)
2 Outside wc	·90	·27
1 All basic amenities	·92	—·46
33 Sharing wc		·98
31 Sharing hot water		·94
35 Sharing sink and stove		·86
22 New Commonwealth immigrants		·66
19 Multiple dwellings converted		·65
39 Households occupied $1\frac{1}{2}+$ persons per room		·64
21 Irish immigrants		·64
20 Private renting		·54
41 Unemployment rate		·48
30 Travel to work		·40

Birmingham

Variable	Stepwise multiple correlation	Simple correlation
17 Migration into local authority	·73	·73
16 Dwelling size	·83	·62
33 Sharing wc		·95
31 Sharing hot water		·88
35 Sharing sink and stove		·81
22 New Commonwealth immigrants		·63
39 Households occupied $1\frac{1}{2}+$ persons per room		·59
19 Multiple dwellings converted		·55
29 Households without families		·55
21 Irish immigrants		·48
20 Private renting		·45

Variables 33, Sharing wc, 31, Sharing hot water and 35, Sharing sink and stove, have been eliminated from the multiple correlation matrix because of multicollinearity.

Source: 1966 Census Ward Data, Base Map prepared by The Centre for Urban and Regional Studies, University of Birmingham

19 Conurbation The percentage of dwellings that are multiple, and converted to that use

Maximum included in highest level only

1	2	3	4	5	6	7	8
0·00–0·80	0·80–1·60	1·60–2·40	2·40–3·20	3·20–4·00	4·00–4·80	4·80–5·60	5·60–6·40

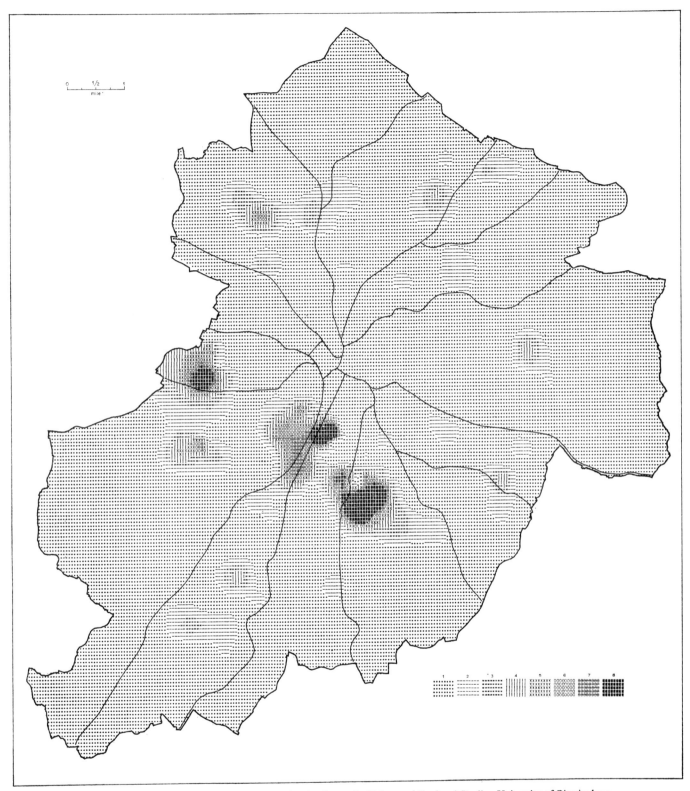

Source: 1966 Enumeration-District Data, Base Map prepared by the Centre for Urban and Regional Studies, University of Birmingham

19 Birmingham The percentage of dwellings that are multiple, and converted to that use

Maximum included in highest level only

1	2	3	4	5	6	7	8
0·00–3·00	3·00–6·00	6·00–9·00	9·00–12·00	12·00–15·00	15·00–18·00	18·00–21·00	21·00–24·00

Variable 19

The percentage of dwellings that are multiple and converted to that use

Purpose-built 'multiple dwellings', blocks of flats and maisonettes, were discussed in Section IV (variable 15), and their association with council house building policy in recent years was emphasized. Here, mainly in the private housing sector, large houses that have outlived their economic usefulness as single dwellings have been subdivided into flats and flatlets. Their general importance is not very great: only 1 per cent of dwellings in the Conurbation were of this type in 1966 and 1·5 per cent in Birmingham. Nevertheless, they exhibit important concentrations in their distribution and the ward values in the Conurbation range up to 6·4 per cent of all dwellings, while some Birmingham enumeration districts have as much as 24 per cent of conversions.

The interest of this measure is derived from the information that it provides about the rehabilitation of large old houses. Conversion implies the investment of some capital by a landlord and an adequate income for the residents in order to pay suitable rents. The distinction needs to be made clear between the majority of dwellings plotted on the maps of this variable and the shared accommodation traced by the last variable. Converted dwellings may in fact share certain basic amenities but many of them are intended to be self-contained. A comparison of the Conurbation maps of converted and shared dwellings shows that there is some association between the distributions. The exceptions are revealing, however: there are very few conversions in the north-western part of Birmingham where sharing of dwellings is relatively concentrated. Instead, converted dwellings are found in marked concentration in Sutton Coldfield and also in the southern part of Stourbridge to the south-west of the Black Country. The latter areas, of

course, are similar in their socio–economic character to the areas of Edgbaston and Moseley that appear on the maps of both variables in the city of Birmingham. They also possess the same type of housing stock in terms of age and size. Thus the Conurbation map of this variable picks out more prosperous areas that appear to have few of the social problems of the 'zone of transition' discussed in the introduction to this section.

The detailed patterns on the enumeration-district maps of Birmingham provide some explanation of this situation and also illustrate an important point about the nature of the spatial correlations throughout this atlas (for details, see Introduction). In the city there is a general association between parts of the pattern of variable 18 and the pattern of this variable, in the Edgbaston–Moseley belt. This simply signifies that the houses in this zone are liable to be converted, shared or both; there is no evidence that conversions in this area are also shared, simply because of the correspondence of geographical pattern between the two variables. On the other hand, the absence of any concentration of converted dwellings in the Soho area, to the north-west of the city centre, where shared accommodation is found, confirms the remarks made in discussing variable 18. The Soho area differs markedly from the southern parts of the city that also appear on the maps of variable 18. There has been little investment in converting houses to flats and this suggests a generally poorer type of accomodation in these areas with the overall emphasis very much upon shared amenities.

This variable seems, therefore, to pick out the parts of the 'zone of transition' within Birmingham that are economically most stable. They are mixed with possibly less desirable characteristics, such as shared accommodation and areas with undoubtedly 'transitional' qualities, such as privately rented

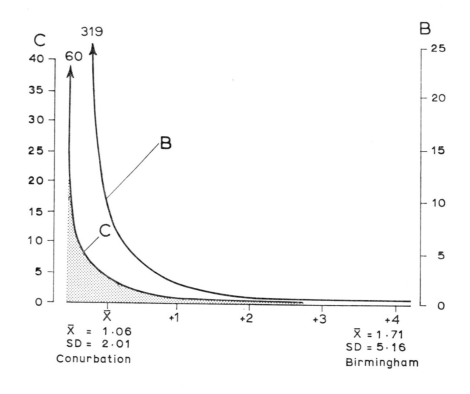

$\bar{X}$ = 1·06
SD = 2·01
Conurbation

$\bar{X}$ = 1·71
SD = 5·16
Birmingham

110

property and recent immigration. The significance correlations with areas of converted property include areas of shared dwellings and amenities (variables 18, 31, 33 and 35) as would be expected from what has already been said. Other correlations include such indicators of relative prosperity as dwelling size (variable 16, numbers of rooms) and high proportions of

service workers (variables 7 and 27) In Birmingham, the proportion of residents that have moved into the local authority within the last five years (variable 17) is significantly related, confirming that we are here still concerned with the 'zone of transition', at least in terms of recent migration from outside the city.

Conurbation

Variable	Stepwise multiple correlation	Simple correlation
18 Households sharing dwellings	·65	·65
35 Sharing sink and stove	·79	·33
7 Professional and managerial group	·82	·34
29 Households without families	·84	·46
33 Sharing wc		·64
16 Dwelling size		·60
31 Sharing hot water		·55
27 Distribution workers		·47
5 Manufacturing workers		—·46
37 Skilled group		—·41

Birmingham

Variable	Stepwise multiple correlation	Simple correlation
18 Households sharing dwellings	·55	·55
5 Manufacturing workers	·61	—·27
29 Households without families	·63	·46
35 Sharing sink and stove	·65	·29
33 Sharing wc	·67	·55
17 Migration into local authority		·50
31 Sharing hot water		·45
16 Dwelling size		·43
26 Dependency ratio		·31

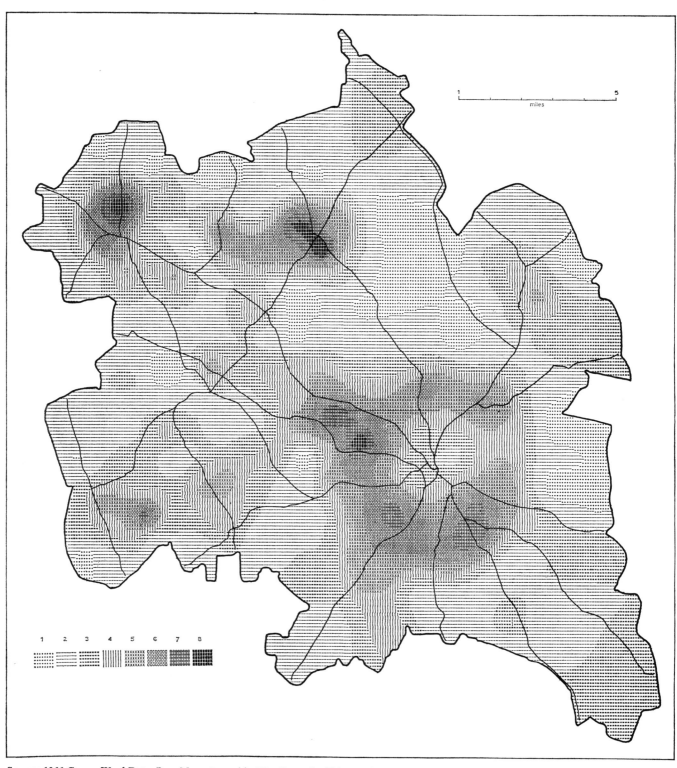

Source: 1966 Census Ward Data, Base Map prepared by The Centre for Urban and Regional Studies, University of Birmingham

20 Conurbation The percentage of dwellings that are privately rented

Maximum included in highest level only

1	2	3	4	5	6	7	8
2·00–8·00	8·00–14·00	14·00–20·00	20·00–26·00	26·00–32·00	32·00–38·00	38·00–44·00	44·00–50·00

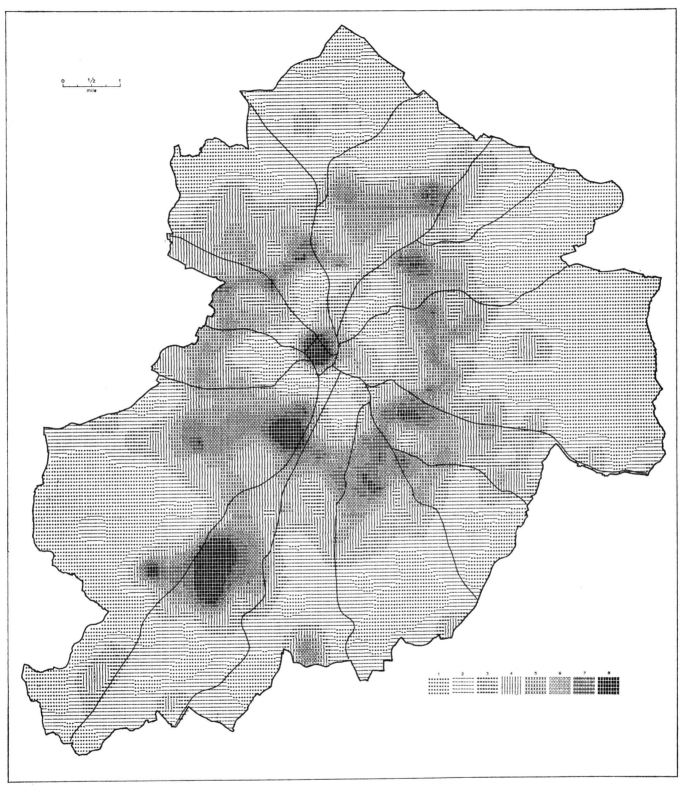

Source: 1966 Enumeration-District Data, Base Map prepared by The Centre for Urban and Regional Studies, University of Birmingham

20 Birmingham The percentage of dwellings that are privately rented

Maximum included in highest level only

1	2	3	4	5	6	7	8
0·00–8·00	8·00–16·00	16·00–24·00	24·00–32·00	32·00–40·00	40·00–48·00	48·00–56·00	56·00–64·00

Variable 20

The percentage of dwellings privately rented

This definition includes all types of tenure other than the owner-occupied and council-rented categories that were discussed in Section IV. For example, as well as privately rented furnished and unfurnished accommodation, it also includes dwellings rented from employers. As we shall see, where sufficient detail is available it is important to differentiate between various categories of private renting. The general significance of this variable arises from its place as another key to 'transitional' characteristics in the areas where it occurs. It is a form of tenure that is usually favoured by certain, rather untypical groups within the population, whether by choice or necessity: single people, students and recent immigrants, whether from Durham, Galway or Jamaica.

In the factor analysis that formed the basis for subdividing this atlas into sections, this variable grouped itself differently in the analysis of Conurbation ward compared with the Birmingham enumeration-district data. In the Conurbation, the association was with the variables that we have already discussed in Section I: with the absence of basic amenities – the 'poor' areas of the old working-class slums. In Birmingham, however, private renting falls into this section, along with areas of shared amenities and immigration. Part of the explanation for this may be due to the higher incidence of company owned rented property in the Black Country, in scattered blocks of nineteenth-century terraces throughout the built-up area. On the other hand, the distinction may simply be a product of the larger scale of the ward analysis for the Conurbation compared with the enumeration-district analysis of Birmingham: the geographical separation of poor nineteenth-century housing from areas of larger houses that are now rented is on too small a scale in the towns of the Black Country to be picked out by ward aggregates. More detailed enumeration-district analysis of the whole Conurbation would be needed to differentiate these local patterns within the Black Country.

In the Conurbation in 1966 there were 109,000 privately rented dwellings, about 15 per cent of the total stock, compared with a proportion in England and Wales of 19·3 per cent. The figure for Birmingham fell between these, at 17 per cent. The range of values in the Conurbation wards was from 2 per cent to 50 per cent, while the Birmingham enumeration-district values varied from 0 to a maximum of 64 per cent. Both frequency distributions, but especially that for Birmingham, were positively skewed.

The areas of highest concentration in the Conurbation (more than 38 per cent) are found to the south of Birmingham city centre in the rather contrasted areas of Edgbaston and Sparkbrook; in Smethwick and the nearby parts of West Bromwich; and near the centres of Wolverhampton and Walsall. At a lower level of representation (more than 26 per cent) privately rented dwellings are found in a fairly continuous ring around central Birmingham with extension into the eastern part of the Black Country and the south-western parts of the city. The Walsall zone is extended to the west, to include areas around Willenhall and Darlaston, and isolated nodes emerge in Cradley Heath and Stourbridge in the south-west of the Black Country. Sutton Coldfield also possesses a modest concentration of privately rented dwellings although their character is probably rather different from the majority of dwellings of this type in the Conurbation except perhaps those in Edgbaston. The general pattern of distribution in the Conurbation resembles that of such variables as the proportions of unskilled workers (variable 6) and New Commonwealth immigrants (variable 22).

As we have emphasized in the introduction to this section, the variables of this factor are most consistently related in the enumeration-district analysis of Birmingham. Relatively fine distinctions can be traced more clearly with the more refined geographical analysis. In the city rented property is found in a variety of area types. Three broad areas of high representation (more than 40 per cent of dwellings) may be identified from the map:

a) the city centre. Here there are very few family dwellings and the available accommodation is mainly in rented flats, hotels and also caretakers' flats. The total numbers must be very small.

b) a more or less continuous zone around the city centre but outside the zone of current redevelopment, now mainly owned by the city council (see variable 14). This belt seems to provide the most general definition of the 'zone of transition', within which there are numerous variations, traced by the other indices of this section. Listing the areas in clockwise order from the north, rented property is concentrated into the northern parts of Aston and Witton on the north; the northern part of Nechells (north-east); Washwood Heath and Bordesley Green (east); Small Heath, Sparkbrook and Sparkhill (south-east); Balsall Heath and Moseley (south); Edgbaston south-west); the western part of Ladywood and Winson

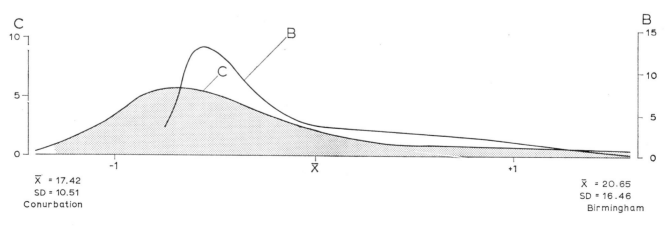

C
10

5

0

-1   X̄   +1

B
15
10
5
0

X̄ = 17.42
SD = 10.51
Conurbation

X̄ = 20.65
SD = 16.46
Birmingham

114

Green (west); and the Soho area of Handsworth (north-west). We saw, in discussing variable 16, that this is the zone of relatively large houses in the city, built generally during the last quarter of the nineteenth century. Some are terraces of 'bye-law' housing, some are more pretentious 'villas' – the local euphemism for middle-class terraced housing of this period – and some are large detached and semi-detached houses, especially in Edgbaston and Moseley (see variable 16). Whatever their type they have been ripe for subdivision by private owners and renting to the groups of relatively unusual socio–economic characteristics that we have already mentioned. Thus although parts of this zone are occupied by recent immigrants from the New Commonwealth (variable 22) and Ireland (variable 21), it also provides housing for students (especially in the south-west of the city) and even professional workers (variable 7).

c) a third and very distinctive concentration of privately rented property is found in Bournville in the south-west of Birmingham. This, of course, is one of the classic examples of a company-built and owned suburb, unique certainly within the West Midlands Conurbation. As we have already mentioned, certain concentrations of company-owned housing on a much smaller scale may also account for other parts of the Conurbation pattern.

The highest correlations in the Conurbation are with the proportions of New Commonwealth immigrants (variable 22), households with no families (variable 29, single persons), the absence of hot water (variable 32) and the sharing of dwellings and household amenities (variables 18, 31, 33 and 35). In Birmingham, similar variables are important in the areas of high private renting, with the addition of high proportions of Irish immigrants (variable 21). Of the more or less permanently settled groups, excluding students and other single persons, the immigrant communities seem to be most closely associated with the poorer aspects of areas with private renting but this analysis does not allow direct conclusions of this type to be investigated. All that the map analysis indicates is that immigrants live in higher than average proportions in areas where there are also higher than average proportions of privately rented property, shared dwellings and shared basic amenities. The figures presented in discussing variables 21 and 22 indicate that there is no necessary direct link.

Conurbation

Variable	Stepwise multiple correlation	Simple correlation
22 New Commonwealth immigrants	·68	·68
29 Households without families	·76	·67
42 Persons per room	·82	−·20
32 Lacking hot water	·86	·61
39 Households occupied 1½+ persons per room	·87	·36
30 Travel to work	·89	·30
36 2-person households		−·66
18 Households sharing dwellings		·54
35 Sharing sink and stove		·50
3 Cars per household		−·48
33 Sharing wc		·48
11 Age 65+		·47
38 Unoccupied dwellings		·46
2 Outside wc		·46
31 Sharing hot water		·43
14 Council renting		−·40
41 Unemployment rate		·40

Birmingham

Variable	Stepwise multiple correlation	Simple correlation
17 Migration into local authority	·57	·57
1 All basic amenities	·64	−·41
21 Irish immigrants	·65	·44
39 Households occupied 1½+ persons per room	·68	·22
6 Unskilled group	·70	·25
14 Council renting		−·58
22 New Commonwealth immigrants		·51
18 Households sharing dwellings		·45
33 Sharing wc		·43
16 Dwelling size		·41
29 Households without families		·38
31 Sharing hot water		·36
37 Skilled group		−·36
24 Fertility ratio		·31
35 Sharing sink and stove		·30

Variables 14, Council renting and 19, Private renting, have been eliminated from the multiple correlation matrix because of multicollinearity.

Source: 1966 Census Ward Data, Base Map prepared by The Centre for Urban and Regional Studies, University of Birmingham

21 Conurbation The percentage of the population born in Northern Ireland and Eire

Maximum included in highest level only

1	2	3	4	5	6	7	8
0·00–1·00	1·00–2·00	2·00–3·00	3·00–4·00	4·00–5·00	5·00–6·00	6·00–7·00	7·00–8·00

Source: 1966 Enumeration-District Data, Base Map prepared by The Centre for Urban and Regional Studies, University of Birmingham

21 Birmingham The percentage of the population born in Northern Ireland and Eire

Maximum included in highest level only

1	2	3	4	5	6	7	8
0·00–2·50	2·50–5·00	5·00–7·50	7·50–10·00	10·00–12·50	12·50–15·00	15·00–17·50	17·50–20·00

117

Variable 21

The percentage of the population born in Northern Ireland and Eire

Immigration from Ireland is, of course, an older tradition than that from other overseas countries so that many British cities have a strong second and later generation element in the 'indigenous' population. Here we are concerned only with those who are first-generation immigrants – those that were born in Ireland. This group includes people who may have arrived in the West Midlands several decades ago, since there has been a fairly continuous movement over this period, with occasional peaks and troughs. Thus a major difference between Irish and New Commonwealth immigrants (variable 22) is the longer period of assimilation of the former which means that new arrivals often have a wider choice of locations to select in seeking relations and friends. In 1966, the Census enumerated 1·86 per cent of the population of England and Wales born in Ireland. In the West Midlands Conurbation, this proportion was 2·99 per cent, amounting to 71,000 persons; 57,000 of these were living in Birmingham, however, and comprised 5·33 per cent of the population of the city. In both the Conurbation and Birmingham the ratio of female to male Irish immigrants was about 86:100. In the Conurbation as a whole, the proportions of Irish born in the wards ranged from 0 to 8 per cent, with a strongly skewed frequency distribution. In Birmingham, the enumeration-district values range from a minimum of 0 up to a maximum of 20 per cent. Comparison with the New Commonwealth figures indicates that the Irish-born do not achieve such high levels of concentration into either the Conurbation wards or the Birmingham enumeration districts. The frequency distribution of the Irish-born is less skewed, confirming that their nearly equivalent numbers are much more evenly dispersed, at least within the city.

The Conurbation map illustrates, in rather startling emphasis, the concentration of Irish-born into Birmingham and their relatively low representation elsewhere in the Conurbation. Most of the central wards of the city have more than 7 per cent of their populations born in Ireland, with an extension to the north-east into the suburban areas of Erdington. As soon as the city boundaries are crossed the proportion drops,

generally to below 3 per cent and only Sutton Coldfield, a part of Aldridge and some areas of Wolverhampton have proportions even approaching this low level. Most of the industrial Black Country and its residential periphery has a negligible proportion of Irish-born, even in areas where New Commonwealth immigrants are significantly represented. It is clear from this map that immigration into the Black Country from abroad is largely confined to the very recent influx of New Commonwealth people while in the city of Birmingham a longer term and more varied immigration has been taking place. The detailed map of Birmingham is even more revealing and certainly emphasizes the misleading nature of data plotted at the large scale of the ward when discussing local situations. The enumeration–district map shows little evidence of massive concentration into the central areas of the city. It should be emphasized that the median value plotted on this map is 7·5 per cent, compared with only 4 per cent on the Conurbation map, so that a much higher 'standard' is being applied to the figures for the city. Thus although the concentration on the Conurbation map undoubtedly exists, the city map is judging the detailed distribution according to the standards of the city rather than of the Conurbation. The Irish are found throughout the inner parts of the city. Some of them are single men and women recently arrived or planning to stay for a relatively short period. The highest proportions are found in a series of nodes, many of them accounted for by single enumeration districts (more than 15 per cent Irish-born) strung along the main arterial roads. They occupy the same general zone as New Commonwealth immigrants (variable 22), although their detailed concentrations seem to be complementary to the patterns of the next two maps, rather than overlapping. The Irish-born are particularly more important in parts of Small Heath, north of the Coventry Road, and in parts of Moseley, south of the city centre. Other areas, including some small concentrations in the central part of the city (particularly west and north of the city centre) and in Erdington on the north-east of the city, probably reflect an attraction to particular communities where there is an existing Irish religious and social presence.

The correlation analysis for Birmingham does not reveal

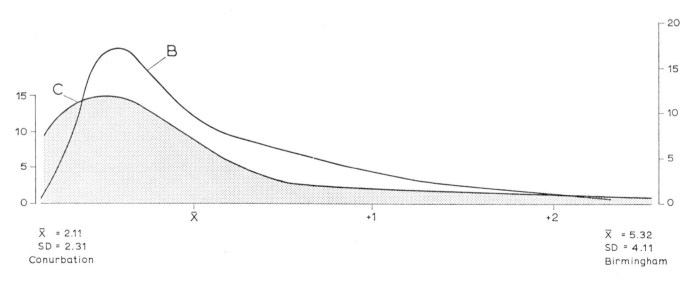

X̄ = 2.11
SD = 2.31
Conurbation

X̄ = 5.32
SD = 4.11
Birmingham

many strong associations, unlike the New Commonwealth immigrant areas, indicating that the Irish immigrants are not so exclusively associated with a particular set of other attributes in the areas where they live. At the more generalized level of the Conurbation, where a much stronger pattern is evident, there are quite high correlations with the use of public transport to work (variable 30); with the sharing of amenities – w.c., hot water, sink and stove – and, of course, of shared dwellings themselves (variables 18, 31, 33 and 35); with overcrowding (variable 39, more than 1½ persons per room), with single persons living alone (variable 29) and with unemployment (variable 41).

Details of the character of Irish immigration are at present more difficult to obtain than those for New Commonwealth immigrants. Movement into the country is generally easier and the process of assimilation has been proceeding for a much longer period and with less obvious barriers. The volume of movement into England and Wales from Ireland tended to diminish during the early part of the 1960s and the pattern of settlement can probably best be explained in terms of a relatively random movement of young workers into the parts of our cities where such migrants can find ready accommodation, either with relatives or friends or in the areas where the style of housing allows cheap rented accommodation to be found. The attraction of the large city, as opposed to the industrial Conurbation is difficult to explain, especially when it is clear that other immigrant groups display such a preference, much less strongly.

Conurbation

Variable	Stepwise multiple correlation	Simple correlation
30 Travel to work	·67	·67
33 Sharing wc	·79	·64
18 Households sharing dwellings		·64
31 Sharing hot water		·60
39 Households occupied 1½+ persons per room		·60
29 Households without families		·58
35 Sharing sink and stove		·57
41 Unemployment rate		·53
32 Lacking hot water		·52
2 Outside wc		·44
22 New Commonwealth immigrants		·42
24 Fertility ratio		·42
25 Mobility within area		·41

Birmingham

Variable	Stepwise multiple correlation	Simple correlation
39 Households occupied 1½+ persons per room	·51	·51
20 Private renting	·61	·44
3 Cars per household	·64	−·45
18 Households sharing dwellings	·66	·49
35 Sharing sink and stove	·67	·38
24 Fertility ratio		·45
33 Sharing wc		·45
31 Sharing hot water		·44
6 Unskilled group		·42
32 Lacking hot water		·42
10 Age 45–65		−·42
29 Households without families		·42
30 Travel to work		·42
22 New Commonwealth immigrants		·41
17 Migration into local authority		·39
37 Skilled group		−·35
41 Unemployment rate		·33
42 Persons per room		·32

Source: 1966 Census Ward Data, Base Map prepared by The Centre for Urban and Regional Studies, University of Birmingham

22 Conurbation The percentage of the population born in the New Commonwealth

Maximum included in highest level only

1	2	3	4	5	6	7	8
0·00–2·00	2·00–4·00	4·00–6·00	6·00–8·00	8·00–10·00	10·00–12·00	12·00–14·00	14·00–16·00

Source: 1966 Enumeration-District Data, Base Map prepared by The Centre for Urban and Regional Studies, University of Birmingham

22 Birmingham The percentage of the population born in the New Commonwealth

Maximum included in highest level only

1	2	3	4	5	6	7	8
0·00–5·00	5·00–10·00	10·00–15·00	15·00–20·00	20·00–25·00	25·00–30·00	30·00–35·00	35·00–40·00

The percentage of the population born in the 'New Commonwealth'

A good deal of public controversy surrounds the influx at the beginning of the decade of a relatively large number of immigrants from India, Pakistan and the Caribbean. The 1966 Census thus made a specific study of Commonwealth immigrant households, as part of its examination of the places of birth of the whole population. The Census showed that a total of 2,478,060 immigrants (i.e. overseas born) were living in England and Wales at that time, about 5·3 per cent of the total population. The largest group is that from non-Commonwealth foreign countries (837,150). Next, immigrants from the 'new' Commonwealth (i.e. the Commonwealth and Colonies excluding Australia, New Zealand and Canada) numbered 829,750; Irish-born numbered 698,600; and those born in the 'old' Commonwealth amounted to 112,560 persons. None of these figures include children of immigrants born in this country. The New Commonwealth immigrants with which we are concerned here thus represent only one third of all immigrants, less than 2 per cent of the total population of England and Wales.

In many ways, the particular problems associated with the New Commonwealth immigrants, as with virtually all other immigrant groups, wherever they find themselves, arise from the concentration of new arrivals into certain areas within the major cities and conurbations. There are a number of reasons for this, as we have suggested in the introduction to this section, some related to the availability of public and private housing during a period of general housing shortage in cities and some obviously based upon the tendency for distinctive cultural groups to wish to live together in the same area. 367,700 of the persons born in the New Commonwealth lived in greater London in 1966, with about 517,000 persons in families

there with either the head of household or his wife so born. The West Midlands Conurbation had attracted 84,700 immigrants by 1966, with a total of 115,220 in their families, and the other two main centres of concentration were west Yorkshire and south-east Lancashire, with respectively 35,000 and 30,000 persons born in the New Commonwealth.

The enumerated figures for England and Wales in the 1966 census include, of course, groups other than coloured settlers intending to live in this country more or less permanently. They include students (of whom about 12,000 arrived in 1966) and other long-term visitors. They also include about 70,000 'Anglo-Indians', of European stock, born in India and Pakistan. On the other hand, it has been calculated (Reference 8, page 24) that the 1966 Sample Census under-enumerated the numbers of coloured immigrants from India, Pakistan and the Caribbean by about 75,200 for England and Wales. This undercounting was concentrated into some groups rather than others: the England and Wales estimate of 175,000 Indian-born coloured immigrants was probably about 4·6 per cent underestimated, the 73,000 Pakistan-born 29·5 per cent, and the 268,000 Carribbean-born were about 11 per cent underestimated. We do not know how these sampling faults were distributed geographically to affect the West Midlands figure, although in 1961, the 10 per cent Census under-enumeration of all Commonwealth immigrants in the region was an estimated 32 per cent, compared with the national average of 17 per cent (Reference 8, page 12). In spite of these errors, the 1966 Census provides the most comprehensive source of detailed data and the form of these computer maps allows the crucial feature of geographical concentration to be examined in some detail. There is no reason to believe that the geographical patterns have been distorted very greatly by any under-enumeration.

In 1966, 49,870 of the enumerated New Commonwealth

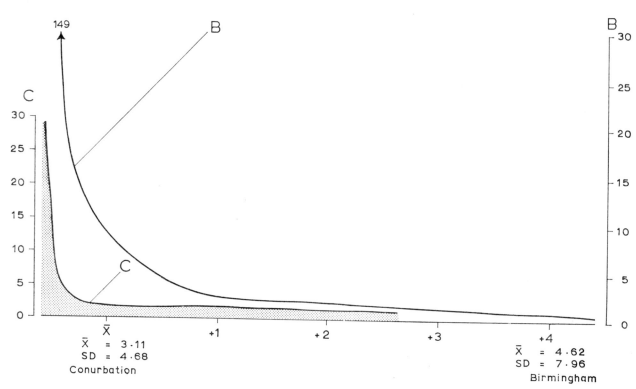

immigrants in the West Midlands Conurbation were in Birmingham. There were over 13,300 in Wolverhampton C.B., 6,000 each in Warley C.B. and Walsall C.B., 5,000 in West Bromwich C.B. and 2,200 in Dudley C.B. 42 per cent of the total number in the Conurbation were from the Caribbean, 31 per cent from India and 17 per cent from Pakistan. Almost two-thirds of these had been living at the same address in 1961 and only the other third had arrived from abroad in the following five years. The main influx of new immigrants took place over the two or three-year period before the Commonwealth Immigrants Act of 1962 and this was in progress at the time of the 1961 Census. Since then an increasing proportion of immigrants have been dependants of those already in this country arriving to join their families.

In spite of this 'balancing up' process in the immigrant communities, they still had rather untypical female–male ratios in 1966: 58:100 overall for the West Midlands Conurbation, with the Caribbean groups having the best balance, at 85:100. Those of Indian origin had a ratio of 64:100 and the smaller Pakistan group had only 11:100. The published census tables suggest that the principal employment of immigrants in the Conurbation is in the prosperous manufacturing industries that have been generally short of labour in the region in recent years. These include metal manufacturing (especially foundry work), with about 13,000 immigrant workers in the Conurbation; metal goods production (about 9,800); engineering and electrical goods (5,700); vehicle production (5,000); and also transport and communications (3,400) and construction (2,200). About 16,000 of the 56,000 New Commonwealth immigrant workers were classed as skilled manual workers in the Conurbation, 15,000 semi-skilled (including one-third of women) and about 14,000 unskilled.

Housing, as we have already intimated, is the most immediate problem raised by the immigrant influx. We have referred to the division between council-rented housing (variable 14) and privately owned or rented property (variables 13 and 20) in the general population. The main difference between this general population and the housing of the immigrant groups in the Conurbation is that only 9 per cent of the dwellings of the latter are rented from local authorities, compared with the general average of 39 per cent. This is not altogether surprising, with a waiting list for council houses based upon length of residence in Birmingham, for example, of 38,000 families in 1966. It means, however, that new arrivals in the city, from anywhere else, depend upon the private accommodation market as owner-occupiers or, for the poorer families and single persons, as tenants of private landlords. We discussed the implications of this situation for official housing policy in the introduction to this section. One-third of New Commonwealth immigrants in the West Midlands Conurbation lived in privately rented property in 1966. This compares with a proportion of 15 per cent in the population at large. Families of Indian origin are least dependent upon rented dwellings which make up only about 19 per cent of their total while, on the other hand, 41 per cent of the immigrants from the Caribbean rent from private landlords. These two groups own 73 per cent and 51 per cent of their dwellings respectively (compared with 43 per cent of the total number of dwellings owner-occupied in the Conurbation).

The groups that we have been discussing here therefore make up about 3·5 per cent of the total population of the Conurbation and, even if their families living within the region are accounted for, they reach a proportion of only 5·5 per cent. Within the Conurbation, there are intense local concentrations, however, and it is these areas that stand out on our maps. The range of values for the wards of the whole Conurbation is from 0 to 16 per cent, while the enumeration districts of Birmingham have proportions ranging up to 40 per cent. In both cases, the frequency distribution of the values is very strongly positively skewed, indicating a high degree of concentration, with many areas (102 of the 161 wards) with virtually no immigrants. The areas of highest concentration in the Conurbation as a whole (greater than 12 per cent of the ward population from the New Commonwealth) form a broken ring around central Birmingham, broadly, but not exclusively within the zone of relatively high private renting already discussed – the areas of late nineteenth-century terraced and villa housing. Smethwick and West Bromwich have appreciable proportions on the eastern side of the Black Country (running continuously into Birmingham) and the other important centres of immigrant concentration are around the centres of Wolverhampton and Walsall, with a belt of lower representation (generally around 5 per cent) stretching between them. The zone of generally poor housing conditions that has emerged from Section I stands out strongly in this map.

More interesting is the detail that the map of the City of Birmingham provides. New Commonwealth immigrants occupy the by now familiar zone built in the late nineteenth century, lying between the slum clearance areas around the city centre and the outer suburbs of the city. Their distribution in 1966 was by no means continuous, however, and certainly not completely associated with any of the other indices that we have used to mark out this transitional zone of untypical socio–economic character. The local situation of the New Commonwealth immigrant communities is quite variable and they are, of course intermixed with locally born families, other immigrant groups, particularly the Irish, and itinerant groups such as students and other single workers. New Commonwealth immigrants are found in particular concentrations (more than 20 per cent of the enumeration-district totals) in the Soho and Lozells areas on the north-west of the city centre; in Aston on the north; to a lesser degree in Saltley on the east of the city centre; in Small Heath and Sparkbrook to the south-east; in Balsall Heath and the adjacent parts of Moseley to the south; and to the west of Ladywood in the Summerfields area, adjacent to Smethwick.

We have seen that quite a large proportion of the immigrant families are owner-occupiers in these areas, but, because of the low proportion of council housing that they occupy, they have an untypical reliance upon privately rented property and comparison with the city map of this variable confirms an association between their distribution and private renting (variable 20). They occupy only a part of the zone of private renting, however – there are clearly many other categories of people who rent from private landlords. Similarly, the zone of shared dwellings (variable 18) shows local nodes where immigrants are concentrated, especially in Soho, parts of Sparkbrook, Balsall Heath and Summerfields, but shared dwellings in Edgbaston and much of Moseley are not also New Commonwealth immigrant areas. Neither do the immigrant concentrations in Aston, to the north of the city centre, and in Small Heath and Sparkbrook to the south-east, have particularly high proportions of shared dwellings. The zones that we have already noted (variables 6 and 16) with high proportions of unskilled workers and large dwellings include most of the immigrant areas but, of course, they include a majority of non-immigrant workers and dwellings. There is very little association with the patterns of the 0–14 age groups (variable 9) or of dwellings lacking basic amenities such as hot water and inside w.c.s (variable 2) – we have already remarked that the sharing of amenities is more common in the zone of immigrant residence. Even the map for Birmingham of people who have moved into the local authority during the previous five years (variable 17) is only partly explained by overseas immigrants of one kind of another: many more people have moved into other parts of the intermediate zones from within this country.

The correlation analysis for the Conurbation and Birmingham confirms this rather complicated picture. Particularly high associations occur betwen areas with high proportions of New Commonwealth immigrants and those with high sharing of dwellings (variable 18) and basic amenities such as hot water, w.c.s and a sink and stove (variables 31, 33 and 35), high proportion of privately rented accommodation (variable 20) and large numbers of persons per room (variable 39). These measures were all found to be associated in certain areas when we discussed the character of privately rented property (variable 20). We have seen, however, that there is no complete association between any two of these grouped variables. The extent to which immigrants contribute towards the general character of the areas in which they live is obviously varied and can be assessed only in relation to the complex variety of these areas. They are in a minority in all but a few enumeration districts, so that the character of the areas is shared in a greater proportion by other ethnic groups. There is therefore no complete correlation between immigrant groups, private renting, shared facilities and overcrowding: simply a higher correspondence than average between the areas where these characteristics are found and areas of immigrant concentration.

Conurbation

Variable	Stepwise multiple correlation	Simple correlation
35 Sharing sink and stove	·72	·72
20 Private renting	·81	·68
39 Households occupied 1½+ persons per room	·84	·66
29 Households without families	·85	·59
18 Households sharing dwellings		·66
31 Sharing hot water		·62
1 All basic amenities		− ·60
33 Sharing w c		·60
32 Lacking hot water		·57
3 Cars per household		− ·56
30 Travel to work		·53
2 Outside w c		·49
6 Unskilled group		·49
41 Unemployment rate		·43
21 Irish immigrants		·42

Birmingham

Variable	Stepwise multiple correlation	Simple correlation
35 Sharing sink and stove	·67	·67
20 Private renting	·74	·51
3 Cars per household	·77	− ·45
17 Migration into local authority	·79	·60
6 Unskilled group	·81	− ·48
18 Households sharing dwellings		·63
33 Sharing wc		·62
31 Sharing hot water		·61
39 Households occupied 1½+ persons per room		·58
6 Unskilled group		·48
1 All basic amenities		− ·45
16 Dwelling size		·44
24 Fertility ratio		·44
30 Travel to work		·43
21 Irish immigrants		·41
37 Skilled group		− ·41
10 Age 45–65		− ·39
23 Sex ratio		− ·36
29 Households without families		·36
14 Council renting		− ·31
41 Unemployment rate		·31

Appendix I

List of the variables used in the statistical analysis

Forty-two variables were mapped and considered in the analysis.
The first twenty-two variables are those presented in map form in this atlas

1 The percentage of households having exclusive use of all basic amenities (hot water, fixed bath and inside w.c.)
2 The percentage of households which have the use of an outside w.c. only
3 The number of cars per hundred households
4 The percentage of married women working
5 The percentage of the economically active population working in manufacturing, construction and public utility industries
6 The percentage of the economically active and retired males who are in semi-skilled, unskilled manual and personal service socio-economic grouping.
7 The percentage of the economically active and retired males who are in the professional and managerial socio–economic groupings
8 The percentage of households with two or more families
9 The percentage of the total population aged 0–14
10 The percentage of the total population aged 45–64
11 The percentage of the total population that is older than 64 years
12 The proportion of males aged 15–64 who are working
13 The percentage of dwellings that are owner-occupied
14 The percentage of dwellings that are rented from the local authorities
15 The percentage of all dwellings that were purpose-built as multiple dwellings
16 The average number of rooms per dwelling
17 The percentage of the total population that moved into the local authority area during the five years before April 1966
18 The percentage of all households which share a dwelling
19 The percentage of all dwellings that are multiple dwellings converted to that use
20 The percentage of dwellings that are privately rented

21 The percentage of the total population who were born in Northern Ireland and the Irish Republic
22 The percentage of the total population born in the Commonwealth and Colonies not including Australia, Canada and New Zealand
23 The number of females per one hundred males
24 The number of children less than 5 years of age per one hundred females between the ages of 15 and 44 (inclusive)
25 The percentage of the total population which has changed its residence, within the same local authority area, during the five years before April 1966
26 Children under the age of 14 and unemployed females over 15 years old per one hundred economically active males
27 The percentage of the economically active population working in distribution and civilian services.
28 The percentage of the economically active population working in local and national government
29 The percentage of all households which do not have families
30 The number of persons who travel to work by private transport per one hundred persons who travel to work by public transport
31 The percentage of households which share hot water
32 The percentage of households which lack hot water
33 The percentage of households which share an inside w.c.
34 The number of employed females per one hundred females between the ages of 15 and 64 (inclusive)
35 The percentage of households which share the use of sink and stove
36 The percentage of all households which are composed of two persons
37 The percentage of the economically active and retired males who are in the skilled worker socio–economic groupings
38 The percentage of dwellings which are unoccupied
39 The percentage of households which are occupied at a density of $1\frac{1}{2}$ persons per room or greater
40 The number of economically active persons per one hundred population
41 The percentage of the economically active population who reported as unemployed
42 The number of persons per room

Appendix II References

a The Planning Context

1 Abercrombie, P and Jackson, H, *West Midlands Plan* (London: Ministry of Town and Country Planning 1948)

2 Bournville Village Trust, *When We Build Again* (London: Allen & Unwin 1941)

3 British Association, *Birmingham and its Regional Setting* (Birmingham: 1950)

4 City of Birmingham, Central Statistical Office, *City of Birmingham, Abstract of Statistics* (Birmingham: annual)

5 Department of Economic Affairs, *The West Midlands: A Regional Study* (London: HMSO 1965)

6 Eversley, D E C and Keate, D M R, *The Overspill Problem in the West Midlands* (Birmingham: The Midlands New Towns Society 1958)

7 Eversley, D E C, Jackson, V and Lomas, G M, *Population Growth and Planning Policy* (London: University of Birmingham, West Midlands Social and Political Research Unit/Frank Cass 1965)

8 Eversley, D E C and Sukdeo, F, *The Dependants of the Coloured Commonwealth Population of England and Wales* (London: Institute of Race Relations 1969)

9 Freeman, Fox, Wilbur Smith & Associates, *West Midlands Transport Study* (Birmingham 1968)

10 Geddes, P, *Cities in Evolution* (London: Williams and Norgate 1915)

11 General Register Office, *Sample Census 1966* (London: HMSO 1966–9). The most relevant published tabulations include:
County Report for Staffordshire, Warwickshire and Worcestershire 1967
Economic Activity Tables, Vol 1 1968
Migration Regional Report for the West Midlands 1968
Commonwealth Immigrants Tables 1969
Household Composition Tables 1968
Usual Residence and Workplace Tables 1968
Workplace and Transport Tables, Vol 1 1968

12 Green, L P, *Provincial Metropolis* (London: Allen and Unwin 1959)

13 Griffin, Donald W and Preston, Richard E, 'A restatement of the "Transition Zone" concept', *Annals of the Association of American Geographers*, Vol 56 pp 339–50 June 1966

14 Hammond, Edwin, *An Analysis of Regional Economic and Social Statistics* (Durham: University of Durham Rowntree Research Unit 1968)

15 Johnson, B L C, 'The distribution of factory population in the West Midlands Conurbation', *Institute of British Geographers, Transactions and Papers*, Vol 25 pp 209–23 1958

16 Local Government Commission for England, *Report and Proposals for the West Midlands Special Review Area, Report No. 1* (London: Ministry of Housing and Local Government, HMSO May 1961)

17 Lomas G M, 'Population changes and functional regions', *Journal of the Town Planning Institute*, Vol 50 pp 21–31 1964

18 Lomas, G M, 'Retail trading centres in the West Midlands', *Journal of the Town Planning Institute*, Vol 50 pp 104–19 1964

19 Lomas G M and Wood, P A, *Employment Location in Regional Economic Planning* (London: Frank Cass 1970)

20 Long, J R, *The Wythall Enquiry: A planning Test Case* (Birmingham: Midlands New Towns Society 1960)

21 Murdie, Robert A, *Factorial Ecology of Metropolitan Toronto 1951–1961* (Chicago: University of Chicago, Department of Geography, Research Paper No. 116 1969)

22 Norris, June, *Human Aspects of Redevelopment* (Birmingham: Midlands New Towns Society 1960)

23 Park, R E *et al. The City* (Chicago: University of Chicago Press 1925)

24 Rex, J and Moore, R, *Race, Community and Conflict: A Study of Sparkbrook* (London: Institute of Race Relations/ Oxford University Press 1967)

25 Rex, J, 'The sociology of a zone of transition'. *Readings in Urban Sociology*, edited by R E Pahl (Oxford: Pergamon Press 1968)

26 Rosing, K E and Wood, P A 'Automated Urban Planning' *Geographical Mazagine*, Vol 42 pp 60–4 October 1969

27 Stedman M B, 'The townscapes of Birmingham', *Institute of British Geographers, Transactions and Papers*, Vol 25 pp 225–38 1958

28 Stedman, M B and Wood P A, 'Urban Renewal in Birmingham', *Geography*, Vol 50 pp 1–17 1965

29 West Midlands Economic Planning Council, *The West Midlands: Patterns of Growth*, (London: HMSO 1967)

30 West Midlands Group, *Conurbation: A Survey of Birmingham and the Black Country* (London: The Architectural Press 1948)

31 Wood P A, 'Regional planning strategies and manufacturing industry – some lessons from the West Midlands', *Journal of the Town Planning Institute*, Vol 52 pp 323–7 1966

b The Technical Background

32 Blalock, Hubert M, *Social Statistics* (New York: McGraw-Hill 1960)

33 Conrad, V and Pollack, L W, *Method of Climatology*, Chapter 9 (Cambridge, Mass: Harvard University Press 1962)

34 Ezekiel, M and Fox K A, *Methods of Correlation and Regression Analysis*, 3rd ed (New York: Wiley 1959)

35 Harman, H H, *Modern Factor Analysis* (Chicago: University of Chicago Press 1967)

36 IBM *Scientific Subroutines*, 3rd ed (Poughkeepsie, NY: IBM Corporation 1968)

37 Jones, E and Sinclair, D J, *Atlas of London and the London Region* (Oxford: Pergamon Press 1968)

38 King, L J, *Statistical Analysis in Geography* (Englewood Cliffs, NJ: Prentice-Hall 1969)

39 Robinson, A, *Elements of Cartography* (New York: Wiley 1953)

40 Schmid, C F and MacConnell, E H, 'Basic Problems, Techniques and Theory of Isopleth Mapping', *Journal of the American Statistical Association*, Vol 50 pp 220–39 1955

41 Shepard D, 'A Two-dimensional Interpolation Function for Irregularly Spaced Data', *Proceedings of the Twenty-Third National Conference, Association for Computing Machinery*, ACM Publication P-68 (Princeton: Brandon/System Press 1968)

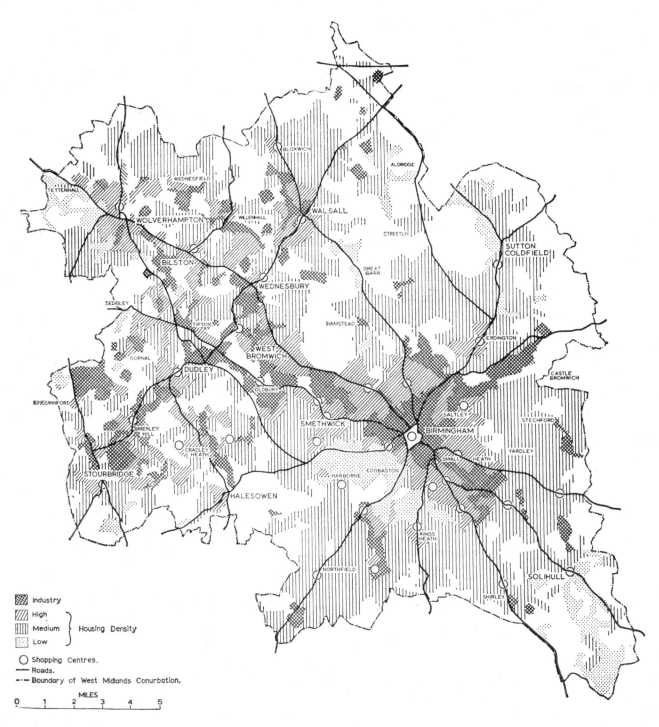

Industry

High

Medium } Housing Density

Low

◯ Shopping Centres.

—— Roads.

–·–· Boundary of West Midlands Conurbation.

MILES
0   1   2   3   4   5

TETTENHALL
WOLVERHAMPTON
WEDNESFIELD
WILLENHALL
BILSTON
SEDGLEY
TIPTON
GORNAL
DUDLEY
KINGSWINFORD
BRIERLEY HILL
CRADLEY HEATH
STOURBRIDGE
HALESOWEN
BLOXWICH
WALSALL
ALDRIDGE
STREETLY
GREAT BARR
WEDNESBURY
HAMSTEAD
WEST BROMWICH
OLDBURY
SMETHWICK
HARBORNE
EDGBASTON
NORTHFIELD
SUTTON COLDFIELD
ERDINGTON
CASTLE BROMWICH
SALTLEY
STECHFORD
BIRMINGHAM
YARDLEY
SMALL HEATH
KINGS HEATH
SOLIHULL
SHIRLEY

Land use of the West Midlands Conurbation